MATHEMATICS AND MULTI-ETHNIC STUDENTS:

EXEMPLARY PRACTICES

Yvelyne Germain-McCarthy
and Katharine Owens

EYE ON EDUCATION
6 DEPOT WAY WEST, SUITE 106
LARCHMONT, NY 10538
(914) 833-0551
(914) 833-0761 fax
www.eyeoneducation.com

For information about permission to reproduce selections from this book, write: Eye On Education, Permissions Dept., 6 Depot Way West, Suite 106, Larchmont, N.Y. 10538.

Library of Congress Cataloging-in-Publication Data

Germain-McCarthy, Yvelyne, 1948-
    Mathematics and multi-ethnic students : exemplary practices / Yvelyne
Germain-McCarthy and Katharine Owens.
        p. cm.
    Includes bibliographical references.
    ISBN 1-930556-86-1
    1. Mathematics—Study and teaching (Middle school)—United States. 2. African
American students—Education. 3. Hispanic American students—Education. 4. Indians of
North America—Education. I. Owens, Katharine, 1942– II. Title.

QA13.G475 2005
510'.71'273—dc22

                                                                                    2004047214

Editorial and production services provided by
UB Communications, 10 Lodge Lane, Parsippany, NJ 07054
(973-331-9391)

ACKNOWLEDGMENTS

The authors express their sincere appreciation to the teachers profiled in this book for their hard work and commitment to improving the teaching and learning of our children. In particular, they thank them for sharing their ideas and responding to many communications. Too numerous to mention by name, the authors also express gratitude to the countless teachers and preservice teachers with whom they have worked for sharing their passion for learning, their expertise in teaching, and their belief in their students' success.

Yvelyne acknowledges Robert Sickles, Henry McCarthy, Jill McCarthy, Helen McCarthy, Mary Anne McCarthy, Daniel McCarthy, Elizabeth Breadon, Wilma Longstreet, Staffas Broussard, Andrew Talmadge, Jay Miller, and reviewers of the book for suggestions that sparked noticeable improvements. She gives special thanks to Lee Stiff for reviewing and commenting on the more troublesome sections of the book. She thanks Lynne Tullos, Faimon Roberts, Richard Anderson, and Kerry Davidson for the expert leadership of state systemic grants that have challenged her to grow in the development of teacher education programs. She also thanks Ms. Laura Fox, who was her second grade teacher when Yvelyne left Haiti to move to Brooklyn, NY. It was Ms. Fox who helped her to feel welcome and loved at P.S. 3, a large public school where no friends spoke French or Creole and no programs addressed the needs of a linguistic-minority child. How Yvelyne wishes she could find Ms. Fox to thank her for the attention and kindness that surely helped Yvelyne achieve her goals as she navigated through new environments!

Yvelyne offers special thanks to her family: her parents, Georges and Eugenie Germain, and her brothers, Gerard Germain, Serge Germain, and Claude Germain, for their love and unfailing support. Most importantly, she extends loving gratitude to her husband, Henry McCarthy, and her sons, Julian McCarthy and Germain McCarthy, for their love, patience, and encouragement, and to her heavenly Father for all He has done.

Yvelyne dedicates this book to her loving nephew, Yves El-Saieh. A "shining star" to those who knew him. Yves demonstrated within his brief lifetime the spirit of love and compassion required to promote a peaceful and joyful world. He lives forever.

Katharine extends special thanks to her friend and mentor, Rosalina Hairston, whose encouragement, vision, and assistance helped to develop her leadership and scholarship in mathematics and science education. For their steadfast love and support, Katharine acknowledges her family: her sons, Jim Owens and Mark Owens, and especially her supportive husband, Clarence Owens, who has embraced her dreams as his.

Katharine dedicates this book in memory of her loving mother and first teacher, Anna Donner. Anna inspired her three children and her countless elementary school students to work hard and to value learning. Initially a certified English teacher, Anna discovered the joy of teaching mathematics to her fifth grade classes and worked diligently to be sure that each student learned well and had fun in the process.

MEET THE AUTHORS

Yvelyne Germain-McCarthy is a professor of mathematics education at the University of New Orleans, where she teaches the elementary and secondary mathematics methods courses for graduate and undergraduate students. She received her B.S. in mathematics and M.Ed. in mathematics education from Brooklyn College. She earned her Ph.D. in mathematics education from Teachers College at Columbia University. She taught high school and middle grades mathematics for 17 years. As co-project director of systemic initiative grants in Louisiana, she leads reform efforts for improving the professional development of teachers. She is a frequent speaker at professional conferences and serves as consultant to school districts.

Katharine Owens is an associate professor of curricular and institutional studies at the University of Akron, where she teaches the middle level mathematics and science methods courses for undergraduate students. She received her B.A. in mathematics at Nazareth College of Rochester, NY, and M.Ed. in science education from Texas A&M University. She earned her Ed.D. in curriculum and instruction from the University of Southern Mississippi. She taught middle grades mathematics and science for 25 years in New York and Mississippi. As co-project director at the University of Akron of the Northeast Ohio Center of Excellence collaborative, she works with university mathematics and science faculty members toward implementing reformed-based instruction in classes for preservice mathematics and science teachers. She consults with the local public television station on curriculum development projects and is a frequent speaker at professional conferences.

FOREWORD

There is a consensus in our nation concerning education that is grounded in the our notion of fairness. It can be expressed in the form of an implication: "If children can learn it, then they should have the opportunity to learn it."

Unfortunately, for many children the antecedent of this implication is either denied or questioned by their fellow countrymen. Many of the African American and Latino students I have worked with in the Algebra Project simply were not expected to learn mathematics—and they were somehow convinced that they could not learn it. But mathematics, particularly algebra, is a gatekeeper subject. Too many poor children and children of color are denied access to upper-level mathematics classes—to full citizenship, really—because they do not know algebra.

The teachers profiled in this work by Yvelyne Germain-McCarthy and Katharine Owens believe their students can learn. It is evident from their stories that they do their very best to give them the opportunity to learn; and, as a consequence, their students are learning. In learning mathematics, students learn that they can learn.

One of the teachers, Lynne Godfrey, is an Algebra Project teacher. In her teaching, Lynne honors how her students think. Like Lynne, the profiled teachers are creating coherent curricula and classroom environments that reflect the vision of the National Council of Teachers of Mathematics (NCTM) for the teaching of school mathematics. They are doing the hard work of thinking about students' minds and experiences when creating ways to approach mathematics that allow students to accept conventional methods of thinking about mathematics. They are using their students' cultural heritages as learning tools; they are connecting mathematics to their students' daily lives; and they are opening access to upper-level mathematics for their students.

It is important to make it clear that even the development of some sterling new curriculum or pedagogy—a real breakthrough—would not make us happy if it did not deeply and seriously address the issue of access to mathematical literacy for every child. Only when all children have the opportunity to learn mathematics in classrooms like Lynne's and her colleagues' in this book should we be content.

Robert P. Moses
Founder of Algebra Project, Inc.

TABLE OF CONTENTS

1

INTRODUCTION

BACKGROUND

In preparing to write this book, Yvelyne (first author) attended a number of multicultural sessions at National Council of Teachers of Mathematics (NCTM) conferences. In one of the sessions, Jean, a Navaho teacher of Navaho students from a reservation school, presented the general characteristics of her students as well as the math curriculum offered at the school. (The names of all teachers in this chapter are fictitious). Although Jean commented on the school's sensitivity to the culture of the students, Yvelyne noticed that it was directed towards behavioral "dos and don'ts" such as the following: "The teacher should not expect eye contact from students before students become comfortable with the teacher."

Thinking that the case of teacher and students' sharing the same cultural heritage should have some beneficial effects on classroom interactions or pedagogy, Yvelyne asked: "Given that you share the culture of your students, are there methods or strategies that you use with your students that you might not use with, say, Asian or African students?" Yvelyne thought it was an innocent question until Jean snapped back: "I don't teach my students any differently than I would any other students!" Yvelyne immediately realized that Jean may have interpreted the question as a negative cultural comment: "Do you dumb down your curriculum for these poor Indians?" Thinking that it would take more than a clarification of the question to get her meaning across to Jean, Yvelyne kept quiet and made a mental note: "Be careful of your questions because some may trigger assumed racist implications."

The difficulty of writing a book on multicultural classroom interactions became clearer to Yvelyne as she stopped random groups of participants at the conferences and asked questions such as "Do you think the NCTM standards *really* work for all students? Do they work for *your* students?" To these questions, Mary, one in a group of three African American women teaching African American students replied, "Some of the approaches don't work for our students. Take collaborative learning, for example. It is ineffective for groups of more than two of our students. Larger groups result in a waste of time. They don't come to us knowing how to work in groups." I mentioned her comment to two African American men, Ben and Dante. Dante immediately said, "That is *not* true! Our students *can* work in groups. They may, however, have to be taught *how*. Beginning with groups of two and then extending to larger groups will help them work productively in groups of four." He then cited research showing how cooperative groups increased achievement of African Americans. His tone and inflections caught Yvelyne's attention more than his words. "I noticed," she said to him, "that you sounded offended by Mary's comment." He laughed at the insight and agreed. She continued: "Should I not write this book or ask such questions? My goal is not to offend people. Can I hope to make any difference, or will I just be viewed as a narrow-minded racist?" Ben replied, "Yes, they are sensitive questions, but they are also good questions demanding thoughtful and difficult responses. Educators need to discuss them openly, just as we are doing now. Go for it!"

Yvelyne invited Kathie (second author) to join her in this quest for two reasons. First, Kathie had impressed her with insights on reformed-based mathematics through the submission of a profile for one of Yvelyne's other books (Germain-McCarthy 2001a). Second, Yvelyne needed help wrestling with whatever issues might arise from the topic, and she felt Kathie's Euro-American background would provide alternative perspectives for discussions.

PURPOSE OF THIS BOOK

This is a book for anyone interested in how the reform movement in mathematics, as advocated by NCTM, is being effectively implemented with students of different ethnicities. Our intention is not to present unique lessons, but to show how reformed-based strategies are being implemented in the classroom. It depicts teachers' and students' actions that unite the goals of multicultural education with the mathematics curriculum. The teacher profiles that constitute the heart of the book are descriptions constructed from classroom visits, written statements, interviews, and videotapes of how teachers implement standards-based lessons in their classrooms. It highlights profiles of teachers across the nation who have gone beyond mere awareness of reform recommendations in mathematics to conceptualizing and implementing new curricula for students of different ethnicities. It shows how teachers implement effective classroom instruction and how their students respond.

Teachers and teacher educators will find the book useful for exemplifying NCTM reformed-based strategies for preservice and inservice teachers. It also provides some answers to a question many preservice students and teachers ask: "Where are the real teachers who are doing this stuff and how are they doing it?"

THE SENSITIVE QUESTIONS

Readers will find that this book provides fertile ground for launching discussions centered on multicultural issues in education. We believe that sensitive questions will arise as readers reflect on the approaches used by the teachers profiled. It is difficult to anticipate all of these questions because we all have lenses tinted by our personal experiences through which we view and interpret the world—as Yvelyne's experience with the Navaho teacher demonstrated. Readers are encouraged to read the profiles and to avoid making quick generalizations about any group since *no ethnic group is homogeneous*; people of the same ethnicity may differ in their history, culture, and language. Yvelyne, for example, is a naturalized American who may be classified as African American. Her ethnic identity, however, is more specific than that because she was raised within a Haitian culture where she spoke only French and Creole at home. Thus, she would classify herself as Haitian-American. Kathie's heritage is German, and she grew up in a rural area of New York State. When she moved with her husband to southern Mississippi, she embraced the diverse cultures (Euro-American and African American, predominantly) of the deep south and used that richness to enhance her teaching of middle school mathematics and science.

We have taken care to present an overview of the students and the school's community so that each profile may be read as representing one example of how one teacher, teaching students within an ethnic group having particular characteristics, successfully challenges students to think about and do important mathematics. Thus, to help eliminate stereotyping of any group, it is important to keep in mind that each profile was selected as one instructional example among many variations. Finally, we wish to apologize in advance for using any ethnic name that may be offensive to some groups. The literature provides little help in selecting acceptable descriptors; we found a number of different names used to identify the same or related groups. Even within the same work we see the descriptors Euro-Americans vs. Whites; African Americans vs. Blacks; Latinos vs. Hispanics; people of color vs. minorities; traditionally underserved group vs. marginalized group or students of color and low socioeconomic students; English as a second language learners (ESL) vs. English-language learners (ELLS), limited English proficiency (LEP) or language minority students, or linguistically and culturally diverse learner (LCDL). We have decided to use the first descriptor given above for each group except when referring to the work of others who use another descriptor, or if a given descriptor is a clearer indicator of a group under discussion, e.g., LCDL vs. ESL learners.

CHAPTER OVERVIEWS

Chapter 2 presents overviews of NCTM's reform recommendations and some of the research that provided the rationale for their constructivist framework. It also describes key elements of exemplary practices in mathematics education. Chapter 3 presents definitions of and research on multicultural education. The profiles in the remaining chapters are of teachers who are successfully implementing standards-based practices with ethnically diverse students. Each chapter also includes a "Discussion with Colleagues" section where we clarify or expand on ideas from the profile; a "Commentary" section that highlights the specific standards, issues, or research that informed the strategies the teachers used; and a "Unit Overview" in a lesson plan format that summarizes key ideas for implementing the lesson. Although the unit overviews specify grade levels or a particular ethnic group, readers will find that the units can be easily modified to fit the needs of different grade levels or types of students. Ideas for extensions of the curricula emerge because of the richness of the activities and because the lessons move from the concrete to the abstract. The profiles incorporate a number of different content standards. They all reflect the NCTM principles for equity, curriculum, teaching, learning and assessment, and the processes of problem solving, reasoning, connection, and communication.

Finally, the summary chapter discusses the vision behind the NCTM standards and what this vision means for students and the mathematics community, both now and in the future. Figure 1.1 summarizes the ethnic group and the NCTM principles and standards addressed in each profile. The profiles presented in this book show that multicultural education is a vision of what education can be, should be, and must be for all students. Join us in learning from these exemplary teachers!

FIGURE 1.1 ETHNICITIES AND THE NCTM PRINCIPLES AND STANDARDS REFLECTED IN THE PROFILES

Teacher/Grade/Ethnicity	Principles	Content	Process
4. Lynne Godfrey: 6th African Americans	1–5	Numbers and Relations, Algebra	1–5
5. Georgine Roldan: 4th Latino immigrants	1–5	Numbers and Relations, Data Analysis	1–5
6. Tim Granger: 5th Native Americans	1–6	Numbers and Relations, Measurement, Geometry, Algebra, Trigonometry	1–5
7. Renote Jean-François: 6th Haitian immigrants	1–6	Numbers and Relations, Measurement, Geometry	1–5
8. Samar Sarmini: 5th Arab Americans	1–5	Numbers and Relations	1–5
9. Diane Christopher: 4th Euro-Americans	1–6	Numbers and Relations, Geometry, Measurement, Algebra	1–5
10. Charlene Beckmann, Kara Rozanski, and Tara Plummer: 8th Ethnicity given in "Commentary" section	1–6	Algebra, Measurement, Geometry	1–5

2

EXEMPLARY PRACTICE: WHAT DOES IT LOOK LIKE?

While I was helping my daughter Helen with her math homework, I asked her to explain why she chose the operation she used to solve a problem. She not only did not know, but also did not care. She was more interested in getting the right answer by plugging in the proper formula. This is how she was taught math, and she doesn't seem to want to change the way she learned it. I can only generalize that this is how many students are responding to attempts by teachers to create conceptual understanding. This age group is where so many students lose interest in math—just when they should be finding the beauty of it. Perhaps I shouldn't worry too much; Helen's passion lies in social studies and literature. She is not a "math-brained" child, I guess. Are these children born and not made that way?

Angeline
Preservice teacher

Like Helen, many students today perceive mathematics to be a bunch of numbers that plug into formulas to solve problems. More often than not, the problems they are asked to solve are not *their* problems, nor do they come close to something they are interested in pursuing.

Helen has two problems, which are indicative of the problems facing too many students today. She not only does not like mathematics, but also has influential teachers who accept this as a natural outcome. What happens to Helen's mathematics learning when her mom or her teacher believes that she does not have a "math brain"? If they decide that it is acceptable for Helen not to succeed in mathematics because she is smart in other areas and that there is no reason to work to enhance her mathematical understanding, then Helen may never change her own attitude about mathematics. On the other hand, if the belief that

5

Helen is not "math-brained" encourages her mother and her teacher to reason that because she is strong in some areas, they should work toward connecting the mathematics that she is learning to her areas of interest in a way that makes sense to her, then Helen has a fighting chance to understand, appreciate, and perhaps even love mathematics. The reality is that every student has a unique and complex brain; our classrooms are composed of many Helens with many varying interests and aptitudes. The National Council of Teachers of Mathematics (NCTM) has made recommendations for addressing the diverse needs of students in today's classrooms.

THE PRINCIPLES AND STANDARDS FOR SCHOOL MATHEMATICS

The recommendations for reforming curriculum, teaching, and assessment made by the NCTM provide a vision of what a classroom influenced by reform principles should look like to reach Helen and other students. In 1989, NCTM recommended that we teach and assess students in very nontraditional ways. These goals are reiterated and others updated in *Principles and Standards for School Mathematics* (NCTM, 2000; hereafter called *Principles and Standards*), which depicts the vision and directions for school mathematics programs. The overall purpose of the *Principles and Standards* is to revise and clarify the unique trilogy of NCTM standards published in 1989, 1991, and 1995 (hereafter called the *Standards* documents) that defined standards for content, teaching, learning, and assessment of K–12 mathematics programs.

Past NCTM President Glenda Lappan highlighted the key components as follows: "What is the reform of mathematics teaching and learning guided by NCTM's Standards all about? My answer is that we are about the following three things: upgrading the curriculum, improving classroom instruction, and assessing students' progress to support the ongoing mathematics learning of each student" (Lappan 1998, 3). Lappan further noted that two commitments inform NCTM's reform efforts: inclusiveness and understanding. All students should experience effective mathematics and teaching, and the focus of mathematics instruction should be to help students develop a deep understanding of important mathematics concepts (3). Support of both commitments requires that teachers believe that all students, regardless of their personal characteristics, backgrounds, or physical challenges, can learn challenging mathematics. It also requires that teachers know how to probe current understandings of students and that they can present students with engaging tasks which may help them connect new knowledge to old knowledge. It is important to note that teachers are to apply the equity principle to all students: "Equity does not mean that every student should receive identical instruction; instead it demands that reasonable and appropriate accommodations be made as needed to promote access and attainment for all students" (12). The theory of constructivism is useful in efforts to implement these commitments because it is practiced or experienced in an environment in which learners are trying to make sense of a problematic situation in order to understand an idea. Constructivism is a framework for NCTM's reform efforts.

Principles and Standards consists of six principles and ten standards that describe characteristics of quality instructional programs and valued goals for students' mathematical knowledge. Together they form the basis for developing effective mathematics instruction within four grade bands: prekindergarten through grade 2, grades 3–5, grades 6–8, and grades 9–12.

Principles and Standards builds on the solid foundation provided in the NCTM *Standards* documents through a set of six principles that address the question: What are the characteristics of mathematics instructional programs that will provide all students with high-quality mathematics education experiences across the grades? Six characteristics, called *guiding principles*, are offered as basic tenets on which to establish quality programs and guide decisions about mathematics instruction at all levels: These focus on equity, curriculum, teaching, learning, assessment, and technology.

Ten standards address the question: What mathematical content and processes should students know and be able to do as they progress through school? Of the ten, five are mathematical content standards that describe what students should know and be able to do within the areas of numbers and operations, algebra, geometry, measurement, data analysis, probability, and statistics. The other five are process standards that address students' acquisition, growth in, and use of mathematical knowledge in the areas of problem solving, reasoning, connections, communication, and representation.

THE NEW BASIC SKILLS

It is important, however, that throughout the teaching of the standards, teachers reinforce students' mastery of the basic skills. In his first address as NCTM President, Lee Stiff (2000) strongly supported this statement:

> NCTM has always argued for a strong foundation on learning the basics. Our vision of basics, however, goes beyond mere number-crunching skills. We hope *Principles and Standards* will help educators, school boards, parents, and business leaders recognize that the new economy demands greater and more sophisticated mathematical knowledge. "Shopkeeper's math" alone is not enough in a high tech environment. NCTM's vision of school mathematics prepares students to meet the challenges that lie ahead in a future they can't imagine" (3).

Hereafter, we refer to reformed teaching of the basics that is taught from the perspectives of the *Principles and Standards* as the "new basic skills."

ENVISIONING REFORM-BASED CLASSROOM ENVIRONMENTS

Not surprisingly, creating a coherent curriculum and classroom environment to promote such reforms is not easy, partly because acquiring a clear vision of the key elements and how they interrelate requires new ways of thinking, as well as practice, guidance, and time to evolve. Teachers or curriculum writers must therefore exercise caution against a limited vision of the *Principles and Standards* that might lead to a superficial or misguided application. For example, look at the following lesson in a seventh–ninth grade class and ask, "How different are the teaching, instructional activities, and student participation from those of a traditional classroom?"

> The bell rings and Nancy's students enter class. They quickly sit in their assigned groups of four and take out their calculators. Nancy's goal for the class is to have them model addition of integers with colored counters. She begins with a review of the properties of integers and their representations with the counters, and then gives each student a package of counters and a work sheet on addition of integers. Students decide who will tackle which problem, and the groups set to work. Nancy visits each group to monitor its progress.

This description includes many of the concepts that we associate with reform: The students are working in groups with manipulatives that include calculators, and the teacher monitors progress. How could the lesson not be reform-based? Let us take a closer look.

> In her discussion of the colored counters, Nancy first defines the use of the counters: a black counter represents a positive number, and a white is a negative number. Hence, three black counters represent positive three. Next she tells students how to add integers having the same signs and then models the example with the counters: "To add two integers with the same sign, just add the numbers and keep the sign. So, (+2) plus (+3) equals (+5), and we can show this is true with the counters." She draws three black counters and adds two more blacks to show a total of five black counters or +5. She next explains how to add when signs are different: "If the signs are different, then subtract the two numbers and take the sign of the number with the larger absolute value. So what do we get for (–3) + (+4)?" A student gives the correct answer of +1, and Nancy then draws three white counters and four black counters on the board to verify the answer. A student asks, "Why do we have to use the counters if we can get the answer by using your rules first anyway?" Nancy responds that this is just another way to do such problems. As she hands each student a sheet with exercises on addition of integers, Nancy instructs them to use the counters to show

the results of their actions. Students decide who will do which problem and begin working. Some use calculators with their worksheet. When most are finished, they wait for other students to finish working. Nancy visits each group, correcting any errors. She assigns different students to put problems on the board when the groups finish.

Our closer scrutiny shows that what looks like reformed teaching lacks key ingredients of reform. First, consider Nancy's use of manipulatives. Properly used, manipulatives provide an alternative, concrete representation that is conducive to students' initial understanding of more abstract concepts or algorithms. They are valuable when introduced as an integral part of a lesson to foster conceptual understanding by helping students see patterns. Nancy's use of the colored counters does neither because she presents them from an algorithmic perspective. Yet colored counters are helpful to students' discovery of the rules for operations on integers. To help students discover them, Nancy would have had to connect her introduction of the colored counters to that of integers as representations of opposite situations using an appropriate model. For example, using a win-lose model translates "+3 dollars" to mean, "I won three dollars," and "−2 dollars" to mean, "I lost two dollars." The end result from adding is "I won 3, then lost 2, so I am left with only one dollar," which we represent as +1.

The concept of opposite numbers follows easily since winning three dollars and then losing three dollars neutralize each other and yield zero: $(+3) + (−3) = 0$. Having explained this model to the class, Nancy could then use it to develop the rules, or she could, at this point, introduce colored counters as a visual approach to operations with signed numbers. She could say, "Let black counters represent positive numbers and white counters represent the negatives. How can we represent (+3), (−2), or 0? Consider this circle representing a set of colored counters where each black is matched with a white. What number does that represent? Let's define addition: to add two numbers is to combine counters representing the numbers inside the circle and then to eliminate zeros. Let's go back now and use counters to find (+3) + (−2)." Once students eliminate zeros, they should be encouraged to see that only one black counter, or +1, remains as the answer. Nancy could then have students practice adding single digit integers that they create at random.

After some practice, telling students to add (+234) + (−456) without a calculator should either get a student to propose a rule which other students should test, or it should create the need for students to find a rule. From this point, students are ready to proceed in an organized manner to seek patterns. Nancy could ask students for suggestions on how to proceed or have students complete a worksheet with a sequence of problems conducive to generating the rules. Once students have discussed and found some patterns, they should test them with several examples, and if "Chris" discovers the rule, then it becomes *Chris's* rule for addition of integers, not the teacher's.

What about Nancy's use of the calculator? Students who are using it as a quick way to merely get the answers to the problems are using it inappropriately. However, those using it to check their guesses for addition of large integers, or to find new patterns, are engaging the full power of the calculator to promote higher thinking. Nancy's arrangement of students' seats in pairs versus in rows of desks may be conducive to small group processing of ideas. *Principles and Standards* recommends that students work in small groups: "This approach is often very effective with students in the middle grades because they can try out their ideas in the relative privacy of a small group before opening themselves up to the entire class" (NCTM 2000, 272). In Nancy's groups, students worked individually applying her rules; therefore, there was little motivation for group members to share ideas. Furthermore, it was Nancy, not group members, who judged the correctness of answers and determined who would report answers on the board. She did not try to assess students' understanding, pose questions to provoke further thinking, or suggest to students that they enlist the help of others.

Was Nancy's approach bad? No, there might have been some educational gains for some students. Learners construct their own knowledge at all times and in all types of situations, but different instructional approaches may influence the quality and content accuracy of the construction. The fact that students faced each other in small groups rather than in rows looking at each others' backs surely promoted some worthwhile discussion among students, but the amount and quality of their interchange in terms of learning the mathematics involved would undoubtedly have been increased had Nancy designed the assignment to challenge students. Although the colored counters were not applied in the best way to enhance the students' ability to make connections between multiple representations, they still provided an alternative view for doing operations with integers, and they may have helped some students to better understand the mathematics. Nancy also had students present their answers, thus opening an opportunity for students to share their thinking and summarize ideas.

We surmise that Nancy's perception of teaching mathematics is one that relies on teacher control or is conceptually rule driven. She probably has had little experience using various tools, such as manipulatives, to guide exploratory activities. However, the fact that she has elements that are conducive to reform activities in her class indicates that she is trying to embrace different approaches to teaching. Her instruction and choice of activities are those of a teacher in transition to a reform-based teaching approach. A clearer vision of what the *Principles and Standards* recommends is a key to her success at moving forward with the transition.

Now let us consider a typical classroom of 30 students who are sitting in straight rows and busily working individually on a worksheet. Claudette, the teacher, stands at the front of the room or occasionally circulates about and looks over their shoulders. Is she teaching from a reform perspective? Maybe. It depends on what the worksheet requires and whether students have opportunities to learn in other ways described by the *Principles and Standards* on other days. Suppose Claudette's goal is for students to apply the heuristic "think of a simpler problem" to nonroutine problems. Below are the examples on the worksheet:

1. Find the last two digits of $11^{20} - 1$

2. Determine a rule for finding the following sum:
   $1^2 - 2^2 + 3^2 - 4^2 + 5^2 \ldots + 1999^2$

3. Be prepared to explain to the class your strategies for getting your answers.

The sheet is not of the "drill-and-kill" variety. It requires students to apply sound problem-solving heuristics to problems that are suitable for individual work. Furthermore, the third question promotes the sharing of students' ideas and discourse. If Claudette occasionally varies her teaching style, she may be teaching from a reform-based perspective.

The two examples above show that labeling an activity or class as reform-based or not requires close scrutiny of the work students do, how they do it, and whether a single teaching method is expected to be used exclusively.

EXEMPLARY PRACTICES

There are exemplary practices that clearly demonstrate the best practices for teaching and learning for understanding. For example, the teachers who are profiled in this book:

♦ Engage students in challenging, mathematically appropriate tasks that make sense to students.

♦ Create a classroom atmosphere conducive to discourse that encourages students' alternative conjectures, approaches, and explanations.

♦ Use appropriate tools, cooperative group work, and individual instruction to accommodate students with different learning styles.

♦ Use alternative assessment methods to assess students and guide their instruction.

♦ Collaborate with colleagues and pursue other professional development activities to support or improve their practice.

Do any of the teachers lecture at times? Sure. Many of us learned from lectures. (Of course, how well we understood what we learned is subject to debate.) Past NCTM President Gail Burrill (personal communication, April 1998) elaborates on perceptions that teachers should avoid when they attempt to implement reform:

We must avoid misinterpretations such as: everything must be done in cooperative groups; decreased emphasis means none at all; every answer to every problem has to be explained in writing; the teacher is only a guide; every problem has to involve the real world; computational algorithms are not allowed; students should never practice; and manipulatives are the basis for all learning.

The challenge is to make choices about content and teaching based on what we can do to enable students to learn.

In his article in the March 1997 issue of *The Mathematics Teacher* about applying common sense when implementing the *Principles and Standards*, classroom teacher Mark Saul echoes similar views:

> So what constitutes "real world?" As a classroom teacher, I have an operational definition: If it holds my students' attention, it is in their real world. If it does not, it is not. My job is to bring more mathematical thinking into their "real world." . . . What about technology? Should we not use calculators "at all times"? Well, no. We should be free to choose when to use them and when not to (183).

As mathematics educators, we know very well to be wary of universal statements such as "For all x, y is true." Both Burrill and Saul recommend that we be mindful that its negation, "There is an x for which y is false," is often true when x represents students in our classes and y represents a statement about the effectiveness of a specific activity or method. In essence, they are suggesting that we think as self-directed learners in the activities and strategies that we select to reach our students. If we do not heed their caution, I fear that education will continue to be entangled in radical movements that stress one philosophical stance over another.

Keeping our focus on all students' learning illuminates the fact that our students are too diverse to be neatly served by instructional methods labeled "Use me all the time!" The key reflective question that should guide whatever approach we take is, "How can we best facilitate students' understanding of the mathematical content in a meaningful way that contributes to their success in the twenty-first century?" Our best practices should align with the answers to that question.

3

Issues in Multicultural Mathematics Education

One of the discussion questions on the class assignment asks if the culture of our students influences how we teach. It's funny that, even though I teach these students every day, I had to think about where they were from or of what race they were. It doesn't make a difference to me whether my students are black or white. I teach them all the same.

Linda
Teacher in Master's program for mathematics education

Further discussion with Linda revealed that her statement was meant to make clear that she displayed no prejudices in her teaching and that she had the same expectations for all students—similar to the Navaho teacher in the introductory chapter. The statement begs thoughts on some questions, some of which may be sensitive to some readers.

Questions to Ponder

1. Does achieving equity in the classroom imply that the teacher must take into account the cultural perspectives of the students?

2. Will all student achievement be enhanced if a teacher employs a standards-based (SB) perspective?

3. Will all student achievement be enhanced if students are taught from a traditional perspective?

Questions 4–6 use Figure 3.1 and require the following definitions:

FIGURE 3.1 HYPOTHETICAL PLACEMENT OF TEACHERS BASED ON THEIR APPLICATION OF DIFFERENT TEACHING METHODS

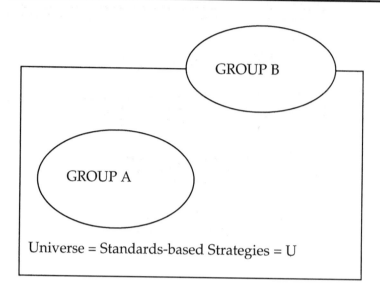

Traditional strategies typically focus on a lecture on the topic, followed by a session in which students do practice problems and then a homework assignment of more of the same. Frequently, the strategies focus on helping students master skills and procedures through rote memorization and algorithms.

Standards-based strategies (SBS) are defined using a slight modification of the characteristics described by Trafton, Reys, and Wasman (2001). To their six characteristics, we add a seventh focused on assessment. Standards-based strategies reflect those that help students to (1) learn a range of important mathematics that includes skills, concepts, and mathematical processes; (2) make connections among important ideas and thus come to see mathematics as an integrated whole; (3) delve deeply into the mathematics through challenging, worthwhile problems; (4) make sense of the mathematics so that they come to understand the big ideas undergirding the important procedures; (5) become mentally and physically engaged in the process of doing and communicating mathematics; (6) link mathematics with application and thus come to appreciate mathematics; and (7) demonstrate their understanding of the content in a number of different ways and throughout instruction.

4. Are there subsets of SBS that work best for enhancing achievement of some groups as in Set A in Figure 3.1?

5. Will all student achievement be enhanced if a teacher uses a mixture of SBS and traditional strategies as in Set B in Figure 3.1?

6. Are there cultural groups, or individual students within those groups, for which the traditional approach enhances achievement?

7. What suggestions do research and NCTM provide?

8. What exactly is multicultural education and why is it important?

Working backwards from the bottom of the list of questions will provide a sound basis for launching fruitful discussions on many of those above. We begin with a working definition of multicultural education.

MULTICULTURAL EDUCATION

The event of September 11, 2001, is but one example of a harsh and painful reality of how intolerance and insensitivity cause death and destruction. How can we, as mathematics teachers, teach children to respond to differences in such a way that they do not become perpetrators of events reflecting hatred of a group of people? Barta (2001) writes,

> Mathematics is a vital aspect of culture. Mathematical principles may not in and of themselves be "cultural," but as soon as those principles are used by human beings, what is done becomes culturally influenced. Mathematics, therefore, is a reflection of the culture using it. We can use this knowledge to better understand not only the nature of mathematics itself but also of ourselves and the people with whom we share the planet. . . . Early in our lives we learn to value and devalue certain behavioral differences and the people doing them. In our mathematics classrooms, we can help our students learn that we all count. What a wonderful opportunity this situation poses and what a weighty responsibility we bear! (305).

We begin by defining culture as an organized system of values that is transmitted to its members through variables that make up one's world-view (gender, race/ethnicity, religion, etc.). There are a number of views of multicultural education. Our preferred view is a "multidisciplinary education program that provides multiple learning environments matching the academic, social, and linguistic needs of students" (Suzuki 1984, 305). As such, it is an educational reform movement that is concerned with increasing educational equity within and outside the classroom for groups of different ethnicity, race, gender, exceptionality, religion, language, and age. In our view, such equity will be reached when *all* students are afforded the same chance to learn higher-level mathematical concepts. It must be recognized that teachers' knowledge and skills are critical factors in determining students' achievement and that the support for effective educational systems by policymakers and the public at large must generate the resources needed to give all students equal access to a high-quality educational experience.

Why should there be a national school-wide focus on multicultural education? It would suffice for us to say, "Because it supports the right of every child to a quality education," and leave it at that. But, for those who are economically minded, census reports predict that by 2050, the minority population will increase and surpass the current majority numbers; thus, as a nation, we must assure that minorities will be prepared to lead, guide, and support the nation. For the maintenance of a strong democracy, the talents of all citizens must be developed and utilized.

RESEARCH ON THE ACHIEVEMENT OF TRADITIONALLY UNDERSERVED STUDENTS

In the past, the academic success of traditionally underserved students (racial and language minorities, females, and students of low socioeconomic background) was not a priority, even though these students did not score well on tests of needed skills (Oakes 1990; Secada 1992). As late as 2002, Schoenfeld remarked,

> Disproportionate numbers of poor, African American, Latino, and Native American students drop out of mathematics and perform below standard on tests of mathematical competency, and are thus denied both important skills and a particularly important pathway to economic and other enfranchisement (13).

A focus on African Americans as a representative group provides a clearer perspective on this issue. In 1994, Ladson-Billings wrote,

> Given the long history of the poor performance of African American students one might ask why almost no literature exists to address their specific educational needs. One reason is a stubborn refusal in American Education to recognize African Americans as a distinct cultural group. While it is recognized that African Americans make up a distinct racial group, the acknowledgment that this racial group has a distinct culture is still not recognized. It is presumed that African American children are exactly like white children but just need a little extra help (9).

We can extend Ladson-Billings' statement to any minority group. Even in the case of, say, English learners, where a different culture is uncontestable, that "little extra help" is often perceived as help with learning English. Yet Moskovitch (1999) reports that "in order to support English learners in learning mathematics, it is crucial to understand not only the difficulties they face but also the resources they use to communicate mathematically" (86). As an example, she cites how the phrase "Give me a quarter" differs in meaning depending on the context (e.g., money for use in a vending machine or a quantity, as in a slice of pizza). To complicate matters, Yvelyne (first author) adds that for a Haitian student, the Creole literal translation of the phrase "Give me a quarter of your pizza" is "Banm ou ka pitza oua," which typically means, "Give me just a tiny piece of your pizza. "

MULTICULTURAL EDUCATION AND EURO-AMERICANS

What about white or Euro-American students? Are they part of the multicultural picture? Should multicultural education be reserved for a setting where there is a critical mass of students of color? We agree with Banks (1993), who writes, "The claim that multicultural education is only for people of color and for the disenfranchised is one of the most pernicious and damaging misconceptions with which the movement has had to cope. . . . When educators view multicultural education as the study of "others" it is marginalized and kept apart from mainstream education reform" (23).

Students in the dominant culture must be given experiences that will allow them to participate in and to appreciate the richness of a world of great diversity. In our view, it is useful but not sufficient to incorporate add-on experiences in the curriculum, such as celebrating holidays from diverse cultures, teaching ancient numeration systems, or adding the contributions of mathematicians of different cultures (Banks et al. 1997). Before students can participate in rich mathematical experiences, teachers must understand diverse worldviews of mathematics, know the historical sequence of mathematical developments, appreciate how cultures have applied their knowledge of mathematics, and come to know and understand how their students learn.

Furthermore, we believe that all students, regardless of the apparent homogeneity of their external appearance, belong to many cultures (gender, ethnicity, exceptionality, or other categories). Instruction must be based on constructivist and situational pedagogies. We agree with Damarian (2000), who reminds teachers that "in the constructivist context, identical treatments are not equal treatments because they relate differently to the prior experiences of different students" (75). In other words, when planning instructional experiences, each student must be viewed as an individual, with the sum total of his/her "culture" taken into account.

MULTICULTURAL MATHEMATICS

Multicultural mathematics is a form of mathematics education that values the culture in which mathematics evolved. Proposed as a potential solution for the low performance in mathematics by students of color, it has its roots in ethnomathematics, a discipline that challenges a vision of mathematics as having little or no contributions from underrepresented groups and celebrates the diversity underlying the creation and diffusion of mathematical knowledge. The term *ethnomathematics* was coined by Urbiatan D'Ambrosio to recognize two distinct areas of mathematical literacy: school mathematics and the mathematics of a given cultural group. The latter area values students' knowledge of mathematics transmitted by the community before students come to school and thus challenges "deficit" models used by the majority culture in its dealings with minority cultures.

Gutierrez (2000) reminds us that "at a very basic level, multicultural mathematics challenges the long-held myth that mathematics is acultural . . . An emphasis on the sociocultural nature of mathematical knowledge also supports a move away from traditional forms of mathematics teaching (e.g., an emphasis on rote memorization, proofs, and algorithms) and opens the door for more active (e.g., hands-on, project-based) and constructivist forms of learning" (204–5).

NCTM AND MULTICULTURAL EDUCATION

In the 2000 results of the National Assessment of Educational Progress (NAEP), Latinos and African Americans continued to perform lower then their white counterparts. These persistently low results are viewed by minority leaders as pressing reasons for promoting reform. (Nearly 500 sample math questions from NAEP are available at http://nces.ed.gov/nationsreportcard/ITMRLS/search.asp?picksubj=Mathematics). These leaders believe minorities have the most to gain from methods that make math accessible to larger numbers of students. They argue for professional development of teachers focusing on a broader repertoire of strategies so that more students acquire the math skills they need. Movement away from the traditional basics and toward the NCTM's new basic skills as described in chapter 2 is perceived as a step toward establishing equity in the classroom by those advocating improved education of minorities (Tate 1995a,b, 1997; Khisty and Viergo 1999; Smith, Stiff, and Petree 2000; Doherty, Hilberg, et al. 2002; Boaler 2002).

In a report on trends in the mathematics achievement of the traditionally underrepresented groups, Tate (1997) outlines the important pedagogical knowledge that teachers need in order to be effective with racial-ethnic groups:

> Equity-related policies in mathematics education should begin with recommendations found in the *Professional Standards for Teaching Mathematics* (NCTM 1991), which call for mathematics pedagogy to build on (a) how students' linguistic, ethnic, racial, gender, and socioeconomic backgrounds influence their learning; (b) the role of mathematics in society and culture; (c) the contributions of various cultures to the advancement of mathematics; (d) the relationships of school mathematics to other subjects; and (e) the realistic application of mathematics to authentic contexts (676).

Are these five recommendations sufficient to change achievement levels of racial-ethnic groups? Tate replies, "Certainly the answer is no, if assessment policy is not consistent with these curricular recommendations" (676).

Teacher Acts Affecting Learning

Although there is growing recognition that culture is important in students' learning, many educators continue to teach on the premise that all students are the same. Some use only one particular form of pedagogy that is described by Haberman (1991) as the "pedagogy of poverty." Haberman remarks that almost every form of pedagogy is observable in urban classrooms. However, he notes that a collection of teacher acts formed the primary means of instruction in urban schools and that "not performing these acts for most of each day would be considered prima facie evidence of not teaching" (291). He defines these acts as a "pedagogy of poverty" that includes the routine in which teachers give information, ask questions, give directions, make assignments, monitor seat work, review assignments, give tests, settle disputes, punish noncompliance, grade papers, and give grades. He rightly notes that, "taken individually, each act appears to be an appropriate teaching behavior for daily classroom life. However, taken together and performed to the systematic exclusion of other acts, they have become the pedagogical coin of the realm in urban schools. They constitute the pedagogy of poverty—not merely what teachers do and what youngsters expect but, for different reasons, what parents, the community, and the general public assume teaching to be" (291). Haberman describes a core of teacher acts, also found in exemplary urban schools, that go beyond teaching basic low-level skills to promoting the critical thinking, problem-solving, and creative abilities of students: "These teaching behaviors tend to be more in what students are doing than in the observable actions of the teacher. Indeed, teachers may appear to be doing little at times and may, to the unsophisticated visitor, seem to be merely observers" (292). In effect, these teachers are modeling the recommendation of NCTM as they facilitate, rather than try to control, learning.

Further Reflections on the Questions

Having reviewed some of the major facets of multicultural education, its related research, and NCTM recommendations, we continue to work backward to probe for plausible answers to the other questions posed in the beginning of this chapter. We bravely present our views as well as relevant research in the hope that they will serve as a catalyst for readers' further thoughts and discussions.

6. *Are there cultural groups, or individual students within that group, for whom the traditional approach enhances achievement?*

What is frequently true of traditional teachers is that they pay little or no attention to students' learning styles or cultures because there is very little variation, if any, in their direct teaching method. They assume all students will succeed in mathematics if students work hard enough to memorize the class lectures, complete homework problems, and answer test-type questions. As for teaching methods, some are using the "pedagogy of poverty" described by Haberman (1991) above.

Some traditional teachers do a good job helping some students achieve both the basics and higher-level thinking skills. Stiff (2001) writes, "Of course, many students are able to make sense of the mathematics when it is organized in a traditional framework. The best of these students are seen as special and talented. Hence, the point of view that mathematics can be understood only by the chosen few is widely accepted" (3). Successful students of these teachers also include mathematicians who resist reform efforts and teach as they were taught because of their own success under this method. Another type of good traditional teacher helps low-achieving students through unconventional measures requiring a deep knowledge of and sensitivity to the students' home and community environments and an extended commitment of time beyond school hours by both teacher and students.

Jaime Escalante, the Los Angeles teacher who was successful in getting a large percentage of low-achieving minority students to pass the Advance Placement Calculus exams and has had a movie depicting this work, is mentioned by Klein (2001) as an exemplary teacher of this type. In the movie *Stand and Deliver* (Warner Brothers 1988), Escalante employs nontraditional tactics to motivate his students. In one scene, he uses his fingers as a manipulative for multiplying by nine—an action that quickly captures the interest of one of the students. In another, he demonstrates his belief that infusing culture in his curriculum will motivate his students to learn by telling his Latino students that they have a rich heritage: They are the descendants of the great Mayans who were the first to use zero in mathematics, something neither the Greeks nor the Romans had devised. He further tells his students that they are " heirs to a great mathematical tradition" and that they can do mathematics because, he says passionately, "It's in your blood!" Escalante really understood his students' backgrounds and made contacts with their families. He used this wealth of knowledge as a resource to get his students to learn. Of greatest importance, he held his students in high esteem for their ability to succeed. In another example of the success of traditional teaching, Klein cites percentile scores at a school with a 99% minority population. The standardized percentile scores for students at that school ranged from 62 to 81 in grades 1–5 (226).

Given that traditional methods do work for some students, the next question is "Why not for all students?" For example, fifth graders in the report by Klein (2001) scored at the 68th percentile. What can be done to help improve the scores of students who score at the lower levels? Does the roadmap lie within using traditional teaching methods? The use of traditional methods to teach students assumes at least three perspectives: First, that all students learn from information given to them; second, that factors such as life experiences, race, socioeconomic status (SES), learning style have no bearing on students' interpretation or processing of information; and third, since no alternative teaching approach is offered to failing students, that it is the students' fault that they are failing and that those who cannot learn in this way are just dumb, lazy, or lacking a "math brain."

Those of us who disagree with these reasons for the failure of all such students have conducted research to find out why so many fail. The research shows results that are at the heart of the NCTM's recommendations: Teachers must teach in ways that recognize and appreciate the fact that students come to the classroom with different cognitive ways of processing information and that their different backgrounds influence how they come to know and understand what is taught. Thus, to make traditional teaching work for all students, teachers need to ask, "How prepared are the students to engage in traditional teaching?" Some teachers respond to this question by blaming of the students: e.g., "They are not prepared; they don't know what they are supposed to know when they come to me." In the case of Klein's failing fifth graders, we know that they lacked skills that were taught by traditional teachers. Because the traditional way did not work, it follows that another option was to change the teaching method rather than give students more of the same. Observations of how students work and process information provide data for this decision. By making such observations, teachers begin to move beyond traditional approaches into the SBS domain. When teachers believe that all students can learn, they focus on *how* their students learn and then adapt their teaching methods to best facilitate the learning. The effect on curriculum is that the teacher's emphasis changes from covering the material for the students to helping them uncover its essential and important concepts for themselves. This approach does not mean that students have to discover everything. It does mean that they are afforded the opportunity to make sense of what they have to learn.

A second option for helping students to succeed in the traditional setting is to teach them the skills they need to succeed within that particular teaching method. Cohen and Ball (2000) call these skills "learning practices"—the different practices that students need to understand and apply in school. For traditional methods, necessary learning practices include knowing how to listen to the teachers' information, copy notes from the board, answer questions correctly and ask questions, follow directions, do assignments, sit in the seat, and study to pass the tests. However, students have been practicing these skills on school days in traditional classes since the first grade! We contend that more of the same is not likely to make any difference.

5. *Will all student achievement be enhanced if a teacher uses a mixture of SBS and traditional strategies as in Set B of Figure 3.1?*

NCTM recommends that teachers use a variety of approaches. Is the traditional method of instruction one of those approaches? Definitely! Past NCTM

President Lee Stiff (2001) writes, "The Standards documents recognize that successful mathematics education programs include the best of traditional and reformed-based mathematics education" (3). Teachers using strategies in set B (see Figure 3.1) may be knowledgeable about the standard and traditional teaching and are choosing between the two based on the needs of their students. If so, set B is the same as set A: Both are standards-based. This question thus becomes the same as question 2 and is answered later. If not, then set B teachers may be in transition from using one method to the other and need more guidance.

4. *Are there subsets of SBS that work best for enhancing achievement of some groups as in set A of Figure 3.1?*

There are subsets of SBS that research reports work well for some groups, as readers will see in the profiles of this book. However, aspects for teaching students from different cultures cannot be neatly boxed under the label: "Look here for strategies that will always work for particular groups." Making generalizations about any group falsely assumes homogeneity of life experiences among members. Using Latinos as an example, Moskovitch (1999) writes:

> Latino students come from diverse cultural groups and have varied experiences. It is difficult to make recommendations about the needs of Latinos student in mathematics that would accurately reflect the experiences of students form a remote Andean village, a student from a bustling Latin American city, a student form a Southwest border town in the United States, and a student from an Afro-Caribbean island. Although these students will have some shared experiences such as some relationship to the use of Spanish, there will also be many differences among these students' experiences, either at home or at school. Both the differences and commonalities among Latino students should be kept in mind when designing mathematics instruction" (10).

There are, however, suggestions from research on strategies that have benefited the learning of specific groups of students. Teachers can start there with similar groups and modify where necessary.

3. *Will all student achievement be enhanced if students are taught in the same traditional way?*

This question is already addressed in question 6 where the discussion suggests that the answer is "no" or "not likely."

2. *Will all student achievement be enhanced if a teacher employs standards-based strategies?*

A number of researchers investigating the impact of traditional and SB strategies on student achievement and understanding show SBS as being more effective (e.g., Boaler 1997, 2000; Carpenter et al. 1998; Cobb et al. 1991; Fuson, Smith, and Lo Cicero 1997; Huntley et al. 2000). Assessments of some the National Science Foundation (NSF) reformed-based curricula (www.edc.org/mcc) also report positive effects on students' achievement. For example, one of the results from the University of Chicago School Mathematics Project's elementary curriculum Everyday Mathematics (Fuson, Carroll, and Drueck 2000) is that their third graders outscored traditional U.S. students on place value and numeration, reasoning, geometry, data, and number story items.

The above research suggests that SBS are effective for helping students to achieve. But do they do so *equitably*? Are SBS effective for all students? Research on whether SBS can promote equity by reducing the gap between lower and higher mathematics performances of SES students has yielded interesting and thought-provoking results. Two notable examples of successful results come from the Algebra Project and the project Quantitative Understanding: Amplifying Student Achievement and Reasoning project (QUASAR). The Algebra Project, a program founded by Robert Moses, helps African American children develop a conceptual understanding of algebra by linking experiences they intuitively understand to algebraic thinking. Further discussion of the project is in Lynne Godfrey's profile (chapter 4) and the Summary chapter of this book. The QUASAR project (Silver and Lane 1995; Silver, Smith, and Nelson 1995; Silver and Stein 1996) posits that low abilities are not the reason for low performances of females, ethnic minorities, and the poor. Instead, educational practices that ignore the needs of these students and make learning inaccessible are the cause. Furthermore, understanding of mathematical ideas and reasoning processes for processing complex problems can be enhanced for all students through SBS. Using six sites that served a socially and culturally diverse population of students, QUASAR teachers at the sites developed NCTM-based curricula and teaching practices over the course of five years. Throughout the years, they documented the process as it evolved, not only for research purposes, but also for its modification for enhancing the students' learning. Analysis of student performance on questions from the 1992 NAEP Assessment at grade 8 showed equitable substantial increases in student mathematics performance.

Not all research on SBS for promoting equity in the classroom has shown positive results, however. We report on two studies that consider the impact of SBS on black or white students from different SES. One study looks at implementing SBS in reading, an area undergoing reform similar to that in mathematics, and the other in mathematics. In recounting her experiences in trying to teach her class of white and black students through SBS for reading (in this particular case, open-ended classroom situations using learning centers), Delpit (1995a) describes her exasperation at the level of achievement of her black students:

My white students zoomed ahead. They worked hard at the learning stations. They did amazing things with books and writing. My black students played the games; they learned how to weave; and they threw the books around the learning stations. They practiced karate moves on the new carpets. Some of them even learned how to read but none of them as quickly as the white kids. I was doing the same thing for all my kids—what was the problem? (13).

Because she cared and believed her students could learn, Delpit then searched for answers and eventually read research reporting that because the norms of SB classrooms are consonant with the norms of white middle-class homes, students from those homes come to school better prepared to learn from SB strategies. For example, indirect or open methods of communication are common in such families, whereas Black students from low SES or working class families are accustomed to direct communication and explicit facts. Delpit concluded that her black students did not have the necessary basic skills to benefit from the open-ended situations of SBS as she presented them. They needed more direct practice on writing skills. However, she firmly rejects the notion that a traditional drill-and-kill approach to instruction is best for minority students. To clarify, she defines "skills" as well as the importance of critical and creative thinking skills for minority people as follows:

Skills [are] useful and useable knowledge which contributes to a student's ability to communicate effectively in standard, generally acceptable literary forms. And I would explain that I believe that skills are best taught through meaningful communications, best learned in meaningful contexts. I would further explain that skills are a necessary but insufficient aspect of black and minority students' education. Students need technical skills to open doors, but they need to be able to think critically and creatively to participate in meaningful and potentially liberating work inside those doors. . . . If minority people are to effect the change which will allow them to truly progress, we must insist on "skills" within the context of critical and creative thinking (19).

Delpit's definition of skills includes thinking critically and creatively from meaningful contexts, so it is equivalent to what we call the "new basic skills" as defined in chapter 2 of this book.

Lubienski (2000) conducted an action research project with 30 students to examine the problem-solving reaction of white seventh graders of different SES to the learning of mathematics through open problems presented within a context and taught using SBS. She found that higher SES students had more confidence and a sense of where to go with the problem. Lower SES students wanted more external direction and often missed important points in the problems. In addition, she found that higher SES students were more interested and persevered when doing problems, whereas lower SES students found the mathematics less interesting than the activities involving games or contexts of interest to them (477).

Lubienski cautions readers not to generalize or conclude that her study of only 30 students implies that lower SES students will learn less from SBS strategies, and she cites the QUASAR project of Silver, Smith, and Nelson (1995) as being effective for promoting critical thinking, discussion, and problem solving in lower SES classrooms. One of her conclusions is that scholars need to be aware that although SBS could improve both lower SES and higher SES students' understanding of mathematics, they could also increase the gap in their mathematics performance. She cites the work of Hess and Shipman (1965), who report differences between the way middle- and working-class mothers helped their children solve problems. While working-class mothers used a traditional approach of merely telling them how to do it, middle-class mothers, using an approach similar to the philosophy of SBS, asked questions to help their children determine the key features of the problem (475). Thus, although she sees algorithmic traditional teaching as dull and ineffective in promoting conceptual understanding, Lubienski suggests that it may be better for promoting equity because it provides "a relatively level playing field by having clear rules and being equally disconnected from all students realities" (478). To teach conceptual understanding and critical thinking skills, she suggests that other means be explored.

Both Delpit and Lubienski report incongruence between the norms of low SES students and those valued in classrooms using SBS. Delpit rejects a return to the traditional approach; and, although Lubienski explicitly suggests that option, she is careful to present other research reporting success in that area so that she can make the point that "methods that are promising for many students could pose unexpected difficulties for students who most need mathematics empowerment" (480).

Can we promote equity for low SES students using SBS? Just as for traditional teachers, SB teachers need to ask the analogous question, "How prepared are the students to engage in SBS?" If the basic content skills are lacking, then the option recommended by Delpit and NCTM is that they be taught within the context of critical and creative thinking.

We can extend this idea to a recommendation that teachers teach students whatever skills they lack as they *keep moving forward* with learning. For example, middle-grades students lacking basic mathematics skills can revisit and practice those skills in the process of solving challenging problems requiring, say, algebraic equations. What allows this strategy to work for those students is the teacher's intention to make basic skills a focus in those problems. Since Lubienski mentioned that low-SES students pay greater attention to problems of interest to them, then a second option is to find or create interesting problems that simultaneously develop critical thinking. If the skills students need to succeed include *how to work* in an SBS environment, a third option is to teach students how to participate in that environment. In addition to the learning practices listed in question 6 for traditional teaching, there are new ones for students to learn. These new skills include the ability to explain and justify answers; to teach to, and learn from, members of cooperative groups; to know when and how to take notes during discussions; to make conjectures; to seek, gather, and analyze their own data for testing their conjectures; and to apply a variety of strategies to open-ended situations. All three options listed above for helping students succeed within an SB classroom are feasible and remain within the domain of SBS.

A fourth option is to use Lubienski's suggestion of having low-SES students study under the traditional approach because it reduces complexity by giving them explicit instructions to well-defined problems. In this case, however, teachers will have to find other means to teach students critical thinking skills. Boaler (2002), in her own research on the relationship between equity and reform curriculum, discusses Delpit's and Lubienski's works and expresses reservations about this option. She writes, "The idea that traditional curricula may be more appropriate for some students than for others is problematic because of its exclusive focus on curriculum. Moreover, the claim that open-ended materials and methods are less suitable for working-class or ethnic minority students is dangerous when considered within an educational system in which many already subscribe to the view that the working-class students cannot cope with more demanding, work (Boaler 1997; Gutierrez 1996)" (241). Thus, Boaler sets out to research how such students can be helped to work in an SBS environment for which they are not prepared.

In 2002, Boaler reviewed her own previous research supporting equity with SBS (1997) as well as the QUASAR and other research. She then questioned why other SBS research that focused on equity, such as Lubienski's, yielded contradictory results. Using Gutierrez's (2002) research suggestions that teachers' practices may be a key for establishing equitable SB learning environments, Boaler designed a study for white, low-SES student achievement on open-ended problems. In England, she studied students from two high schools in a low-income area where underachievers and overachievers were equally divided across SES. Teachers from one school of about 100 of her subjects were knowledgeable about and had been applying SBS for two years. The other school of about 200 subjects used the traditional method.

Rather than focusing on curriculum, Boaler focused her research on the *particular* practices of teaching and learning in the classroom environment, and she examined whether equity can be achieved with low-SES students' having teachers who explicitly teach the learning practices necessary for working with open-ended problems. Among the strategies the teachers used were (1) helping students understand what the question demanded and having them restate the problem in their own words, (2) teaching students to see the value of communication and justification in writing, and (3) discussing with them ways of interpreting questions in context. At the end of three years, the results of assessments that included a national exam showed that SBS students not only outperformed the traditional control students, but also scored higher than the national average. In addition, whereas boys scored higher than girls in the traditional group, there were no gender disparities in the SBS group. Thus, Boaler's results are in direct contrast to the idea that "the algorithmic mode of instruction might provide a relatively level playing field" (Lubienski 2000, 478). Boaler concludes that studies involving relational analysis of equity must not stop at the curriculum but extend to the teaching and learning practices of teachers, which she perceives as central to the attainment of equality (239).

And now, let us address our final question:

1.   *Does achieving equity in the classroom imply that the teacher must take into account the cultural perspectives of the students?*

This question is discussed in the Summary chapter and is based on Charlene Beckmann's profile, which provides no information on the ethnicity of the students before the Commentary section. Readers are challenged to guess the students' culture from the teacher and student actions as well as the types of problem-solving activities in the lesson.

We close this chapter with a definition of culturally relevant teaching which is used by teachers in this book. *Culturally relevant teaching* is a term that acknowledges that all subjects exist within a cultural environment and that culture influences learning. Ladson-Billings (1997), who first introduced the term, clarifies the meaning:

> The notion of "cultural relevance" moves beyond language to include other aspects of student and school culture . . . . Specifically, culturally relevant teaching is a pedagogy that empowers students intellectually, socially, emotionally, and politically by using cultural referents to impart knowledge, skills and attitudes. These cultural referents are not merely vehicles for bridging or explaining the dominant culture; they are aspects of the curriculum in their own right (17–18).

In the profiles presented in the remaining chapters, we see diverse students and their teachers participating in a learning environment recommended by NCTM and the research reported in this chapter.

4

LYNNE GODFREY:
AFRICAN AMERICANS
AND THE ALGEBRA
PROJECT

Young Achievers' 315 students in grades K–8 come from all neighbor-hoods in Boston. The student population is approximately 55% Black, 20% White, 2% Asian, and 20% Hispanic. Because the Algebra Project curriculum is designed around kid-culture, I have great success using it with the students. It's the Algebra Project push that says, "Find the ex-perience that students have, so that they all have a place to enter in." They all bring something to the table whether it's an experience they had before or one that they are creating new. The student's voice is so impor-tant. And once students hear themselves voicing their ideas in the class they are never the same afterwards.

Lynne Godfrey
The Young Achievers Science and Mathematics Pilot School
Dorchester, MA.

Teacher, curriculum writer, professional development provider, and mentor, mathematics educator Lynne Godfrey teaches sixth grade at the Young Achiev-ers Science and Mathematics Pilot School (YA), an innovative citywide Boston Public School. Since its inception in 1995, YA has been dedicated to creating an exceptional teaching and learning environment in which science and mathe-matics concepts, explored by new technologies, are central to teacher and stu-dent inquiry. In collaboration with families, students, community members, and community institutions, a democratic participatory process governs the school. Social justice through academic excellence for the diverse student body enrolled in YA is the collective commitment of all school personnel.

YA can be proud of its promotion rate of approximately 95%, an attendance rate of about 96%, a 0% annual dropout rate, and no pupils suspended. Class size is kept small at about 20 students. Students with disabilities are educated in the same setting as their general education peers. The program of study at YA emphasizes rigorous interdisciplinary science and mathematics lessons designed to prepare all students to successfully complete the college preparatory mathematics sequence in high school.

For six years, Lynne was a full-time teacher in Cambridge. Then, in the mid-1980s she began her role as a teacher resource person for the district, giving staff support in mathematics instruction and teaching one mathematics class each year. Her work with the Algebra Project started over ten years ago. In the school year 2001–2002, Lynne was upper school (grades 4–8) coordinator and mathematics coach at Young Achievers, as well as a sixth grade mathematics teacher.

Lynne's classroom is a busy place, buzzing with the activity of 22 sixth graders whose desks are arranged in groups of 2–3. Chart papers with key phrases and summaries from past lessons are evident around the room. A chalkboard and open area in the front of the classroom provide places for students to share their thinking about mathematical problems with their peers. Graduate student intern Amani Allen works one-on-one with the students and, at the same time, learns how to teach the Algebra Project curriculum.

As I (Katharine, second author) watched the video of Yvelyne's experience in Lynne's class, I perceived that this visit would be like no other I had seen in the many years that I have observed mathematics teachers at work. Almost instantly, Yvelyne was swept into the community which Lynne and her learners had become. Even before Yvelyne made her way to the back of the room with the video equipment, Lynne introduced her to the students and explained her purpose for being there. This introduction was not uncommon; typically, teachers announce to the class that a visitor will be joining them and the purpose of the visit. What followed next convinced me that this visit would be different. Turning to Yvelyne, one by one, the students introduced themselves by giving their names; several added, "Welcome to our class, Dr. McCarthy." To the reader, this behavior may seem trivial, but to me, the observer of the visit, it spoke volumes about Lynne's classroom climate and the priority she puts on the contribution of each person to the functioning of the learning community.

ENGAGING STUDENTS

Lynne begins the lesson, which uses information about the Chinese Zodiac, by directing students to answer the warm-up questions written on the board:

WARM-UP

Task 1:   The year 2002 is a year of the horse. How do you know?

Task 2:   Use division form A, which states that Dividend = Quotient × Divisor + Remainder, to write an equation for 2002.

Task 3:   What will be the next year of the horse? Explain/Show.

Each student has a placemat on which is a drawing of the Chinese Zodiac showing the twelve animals of the zodiac in symbol form (used frequently as placemats in Chinese restaurants). The symbols are arranged in a large circle on the mat; and, with each animal, there is a list of corresponding years in the 20th century of their occurrence in the calendar (see Figure 4.1).

FIGURE 4.1 THE CHINESE ZODIAC

Year Charts

Twelve animals rule a particular year in rotation. In addition to lending characteristics to people born during that year, the animal also influences the quality of a particular year. So according to Chinese Astrology, knowing which animal rules a future year can help you plan in advance for the trials and triumphs that that year may bring.

Animal Signs and Birth Years	
Rat	1996–1984–1972–1960–1948–1936–1924
Ox	1997–1985–1973–1961–1949–1937–1925
Tiger	1998–1986–1974–1962–1950–1938–1926
Rabbit	1999–1987–1975–1963–1951–1939–1927
Dragon	1988–1976–1964–1952–1940–1928
Snake	1989–1977–1965–1953–1941–1929
Horse	1990–1978–1966–1954–1942–1930
Goat	1991–1979–1967–1955–1943–1931
Monkey	1992–1980–1968–1956–1944–1932
Rooster	1993–1981–1969–1957–1945–1933–1921
Dog	1994–1982–1970–1958–1946–1934–1922
Pig	1995–1983–1971–1959–1947–1935–1923

After a couple of minutes, Lynne asks for a volunteer to share the answer to the first question. Steven comes to the board and, holding his mat so that his classmates can see the circle, points to the symbol of the horse. He reads the dates of the years of the horse (see Figure 4.1) and then writes on the board 1930, 1942, 1954, 1966, 1978, and 1990. He then explains, "I looked at it and noticed that if I added 12 to 1930, I got 1942. Every time I added 12 to a year, I got the next year." He takes the chalk and connects pairs of years, writing +12 with each pair. "So I added 12 to 1990 and came up with 2002."

The following dialogue reveals the various ways in which students begin to develop strategies to solve the problem:

Stasha: I have a different way.

Lynne: Come to the front of the class and show us.

Stasha: I looked at the year of the horse and saw 1990, so I counted all the way around the circle, 1991, 1992, 1993, until I got to the year of the horse again. That's when I got to 2002. (*Stasha demonstrates using her placemat.*)

Lynne: Now we've found two methods. Is there another one?

Samantha: I looked at the latest date, the largest number (1999), the rabbit. Then I went to the tiger (1998). That was less, so I went forward and counted around until I got to 2002, which ended up on the horse.

Lynne: So I see a counting-on strategy, a similar strategy to what Stasha used. But, Samantha, it was a little less counting than what Stasha did because you started at 1999 and she started at 1990. Any other way?

As Marcus comes forward, Lynne comments, "These brains are warm today!"

Marcus: OK, first I took 2002 (*he writes 2002 in large numbers on the board*). Then I divided it by 12. I divided it by 12 because in our book we had divided other years by 12."

Note: In an earlier lesson when students first explored the Chinese Zodiac and looked for patterns in the years, they were encouraged to try dividing the years by 12. Marcus shows his division in a step-by-step process, mentioning each use of multiplication and subtraction along the way. In the end, he points to his answer of 166 remainder 10.

Marcus: So the remainder of 10 tells me that it is the year of the horse because that's what we did before.

Marcus points to a chart made by the students when they were figuring out remainders of each year on the placemat divided by 12. Other years of the horse, when divided by 12 gave remainders of 10.

Lynne: Will any year divided by 12, where the remainder is 10, be a year of the horse? Does anybody know whether that's true or not?

Wanda: Yes. It's true because it says on the chart what the year of the horse is when the remainder is 10.

Lynne: So if I got a remainder of 7, what year would it be?

Several students: Rabbit.

Lynne: Good. Ivan, you've got another way?

Ivan writes 166 r 10 on the board. Before going on, Lynne asks him to explain where he got these numbers. Ivan tells her that he did the same thing that Marcus did. Next on the board he multiplies 166 times 12, showing each step along the way. Pointing to 1992, he adds the remainder of 10 and then gets to 2002.

Lynne: Thank you, Ivan. This is something I see Tymesha do a lot. It's called a check of the work. You figured it out like Marcus and then showed us how to check your answer. You didn't just figure it out; you made certain. Great. How about someone for the second warm-up on the board? That's writing the equation in division form A. Courtney?

Courtney writes "12 = 166 × 2002 + 10" on the board and steps aside. Lynne, recognizing Courtney's error and wanting her to look at the reasonableness of her answer, asks Courtney to explain what she wrote.

Courtney: I wrote the equation in division form A.

Lynne: Yes, that's division form A. Tell me about your equation.

Courtney reads her equation from left to right. Lynne invites her to rework the division problem that she solved and adds, "I hear some classmates say they have some problem with what you wrote for your equation." Then Lynne turns to the class and remarks, "But maybe Courtney will figure this out." Courtney proceeds to write her long division calculation on the board (2002 ÷ 12), gets an answer of 166 r 10, and then labels each number in the equation: 2002 = divisor; 10 = remainder; 166 = quotient; 12 = dividend.

Dividend		Quotient		Divisor		Remainder
12	=	166	×	2002	+	10

Noticing that Courtney has confused which numbers are the dividend and the divisor, Lynne asks her to look at her long division calculation, label each number in it, and explain her labels as she's doing it. As Courtney starts to label 12 as the dividend, she realizes her mistake and says, "Oops!" She switches the 12 and the 2002 in her equation and is satisfied that her labels are correct.

Dividend		Quotient		Divisor		Remainder
2002	=	166	×	12	+	10

Lynne: Now I know what all the confusion was about in your first answer.

Moving on, Lynne returns to helping students discover patterns.

Lynne: So when's the next year of the horse, and how do you know that?

Cherese: 2002.

Lynne: When's the next? When will it cycle around again so we'll have the next time to say, "Happy New Year, it's the year of the horse."?

Anthony: 2014.

Lynne: And how do we know that?

Anthony: It goes around by 12; I added 12.

Moving her hand around in a broad circle to dramatize, Lynne says, "Yes, it's a cycle that goes around in twelve's."

GROUP WORK

Lynne transitions to the next part of the lesson by telling her students that they will be doing three tasks in their teams in order to get ready to play the winding game. She smiles and adds, "This is a very good year for many of us in this classroom." One student asks why, but Lynne does not answer and proceeds to write the three tasks on the board as a warm up exercise:

1. Check the work that we completed yesterday.

2. Draw pictures for the three Chinese Zodiac signs that your team was assigned.

3. Complete the equivalence chart (see Figure 4.2)

About a minute later Simone points to a graph depicting birthday data collected by the class. The graph shows that about half of the class was born in 1990, a previous year of the horse. Thus, 2002 is a special year for those students. While Lynne continues to write, Wanda asks, "So in China are they celebrating the New Year today?"

Lynne explains that the actual celebration was the day before and then goes on to tell the class that last night a friend of hers went to a Chinese restaurant where they gave everyone a small red envelope to celebrate. Each envelope had a brand new one-dollar bill in it. The students want to leave immediately to get their red envelopes! Lynne quickly adds that the celebration *was* last night. A mixture of sighs and chuckles can be heard through the classroom. Her story prompts the students to share their experiences eating Chinese foods, using chopsticks, and going to Chinese restaurants. Lynne lets the conversations go on for another minute, then calls Jose to come to the front of the room to lead the class in the twelve-table chant. With a rhythmic clapping, the students recite, "One times twelve equals twelve, two times twelve equals twenty-four, . . ."

Energized to start the three assigned tasks, the students move to their pre-arranged groups to begin. Groups sit at tables in the room or push desks together to make a table. Each student has a set of worksheets and access to a calculator, if needed. Students are permitted to leave their group to work out a problem on the board. There is a lot of give and take among the students as they exchange ideas and procedures, correct each other's mistakes, and give each other help. Lynne and her assistant circulate around the room to monitor activities as the students work. I observed Yvelyne, the visitor to the class, drawn into being an active participant. The group sitting nearest to the camera had been eyeing Yvelyne's note taking throughout the lesson. When the group work began they were eager for her to join them, as a peer, not as an authority.

Typical of the group work is Group A, consisting of three girls and two boys. They quickly finish checking yesterday's work. For the next task, Michelle emerges as the leader, assigning the drawings of a tiger, rabbit, and a goat, one to each of three group members. Marcus, the drawer of the goat is perplexed about how to draw his animal. Lynne intervenes at this point and tells him that any way he wants to draw the goat—either a picture or a symbol—is fine. Tymesha and Michelle work on the equivalence chart, a grid that students will discover places each of the numbers from 12 through 144 in a class from 0–11 depending on the remainder that results when dividing the number by 12 (Figure 4.2). Ivan holds up his picture of the tiger to ask his group's approval.

FIGURE 4.2 CHINESE ZODIAC EQUIVALENCE CHART

EQUIVALENCE CLASSES

0	1	2	3	4	5	6	7	8	9	10	11
12											
			27								
						42					
				52							
60											
					77						
		86									
									105		
											119
				124							
							139				
144											

After a few minutes, the group tackles the equivalence chart but seems uncertain about how to proceed. Lynne asks them to look across the top of the chart (labeled "Equivalence Classes") and to notice where the number twelve is located. She suggests that they find the pattern going across the chart to fill in the rows and to keep filling in until they reach 144. Michelle recognizes that 24 should go into the box below 12, and Lynne presses her to figure out how to fill in the numbers between 12 and 24. Tymesha asks if she can use a calculator to divide and then fill in the chart. Lynne replies, "Yes, you could, but you'll get a decimal remainder, and then you'll have to figure out what the remainder is as a whole number." Michelle sees the pattern, begins to fill in her chart, and then shows Tymesha and the other team members how to get started on their charts. Making sure that everyone in this group has caught on to task 3, Lynne makes one last check of the other groups, collects each group's zodiac drawings, and prepares the classroom for the Winding Game to follow.

THE WINDING GAME

Lynne and her assistants set up twelve chairs in a circle. On the chairs they have taped the pictures of the animals that the students drew in their groups. Each chair has a different animal, and the animals are arranged according to the circle of the zodiac. Lynne sends the students back to their desks and asks them to bring their books when they gather around the chairs. The class quiets when Lynne raises her hand. She directs Stasha to read the set up for practicing for the Winding Game (see Figure 4.3). Lynne points out that she has prepared cards for numbers from 1 through 70 instead of through 144. Some teams will have 6 players instead of 5, and the game will have 6 rounds, meaning that one person in the teams of 5 will have to take two turns.

FIGURE 4.3 THE CHINESE ZODIAC AND THE WINDING GAME

Practicing for the Winding Game

Class Work: The class should practice the Winding Game as described below.

The set up for the practice:

1. Set of 12 chairs in a circle in the middle of the room.

2. Put a picture of a different zodiac sign on each chair, together with its remainder.

3. Put the pictures and remainders in order from 0 to 11.

4. Prepare a pack of numbers from 0 to 144.

5. Divide the class into teams of 5 players each.

6. Set up a strategy desk in the front of the room with paper and pencils.

From The Algebra Project Inc. Transition Curriculum, Unit 2, Lesson 5, p. 57; with permission.

Lynne then describes the game to the class: "Now I'm going to ask you to watch very carefully as I demonstrate the game. I want to see if you can figure it out. I am going to pick a number from the pile and put it in my pocket after I look at it. I want you to guess my number. Now you'll have to watch very carefully. I'm going to walk around the circle and then sit down. The thing that will help you to know my number is division form A. That will help you. And remember to watch very closely."

Starting at the monkey chair, Lynne walks around the circle two times and then sits down on the chair with the dog drawing on it. "Now raise your hand if you think you can tell me what my number is—the number in my pocket." Lynne makes no comment or change of expression as the students share their guesses—2, 22, 24, 2, 26, 7, 2, 26. Some students have no guess. Lynne offers a hint, "I am the dividend." Several students exclaim, "Oh, I think I get it." When Lynne asks once more and a student guesses 22, Lynne tells the class that she is going to do the walk again and that they should watch closely. As Lynne walks, she reminds the students, "My number is the dividend." Lynne completes her second walk, and more students' hands shoot up with confidence to guess Lynne's number. Without taking any guesses, Lynne asks Steven to model the game.

Lynne tells the class, "I'm going to give Steven his number, and he'll model the game." Ivan tells Lynne that he is not certain how Steven will know how many times to walk around the circle. Lynne suggests that dividing by twelve may give him a hint and that he should watch very carefully during this next round. While Steven is getting his number, student-talk, such as "I get it—I don't get it," can be heard throughout the room.

Lynne positions Steven in front of the monkey chair and tells the class that he is ready. Steven signals to the class that he is starting and walks twice around the circle, stopping at the pig. This time there are more "Oh, I get it" replies filling the room than before. Lynne calls on Marcus, who announces, "27!" Acknowledging this correct answer, Lynne asks the students to write Steven's number in division form A. Katherine reads hers: "$27 = 2 \times 12 + 3$." Lynne writes this equation on the board and asks the students to verify that this is the equation they also wrote in their notebooks.

Lynne returns to Stasha and asks her to read the instructions for practicing the Winding Game (see Figure 4.4). Before moving on, Lynne asks, "What is the mathematical name for the winding number, the number that tells you how many complete revolutions to go around?" Lynne presses the class for answers until she is certain that students recognize the winding number as the quotient. Then she poses, "What's another word for residue?" Estelle volunteers, "The remainder." "So what do you call the number you were given?" asks Lynne. Diego remembers, "The dividend. And the twelve is the number we're dividing by."

FIGURE 4.4 WINDING GAME INSTRUCTIONS

Instructions for practicing the Winding Game:

1. A player picks a number out of a hat. The player doesn't tell the number to anyone except the teacher. Suppose the number 38 is picked.

2. The player goes to the strategy desk to figure out how many laps s/he will have to go around the circle and how many chairs will be left over. Since s/he picked the number 38, s/he could just walk around the circle counting chairs until s/he gets to the number 38. Or, s/he could use a strategy to wind around the circle (walking quickly without counting the chairs).

3. The player always starts at the monkey (zero) chair, and goes around until s/he gets to the correct chair. By starting at the monkey chair and walking around the circle, the player gets to the number 38 by counting each chair. Or, s/he winds around the circle, passing the monkey chair 3 times, counts 2 more chairs, and sits down in the second chair.

4. Each student records the winding number (how many times the student passes the monkey chair) and the residue number (the number on the chair where the student sits after the last time s/he passes the monkey chair). In our example, the winding number is 3. The residue number is 2.

5. Each student uses Division Form A to write a division equation that represents his/her observation of the player's turn.

Division Form A:

$$\text{Dividend} = (\text{Quotient} \times \text{Divisor}) + \text{Remainder}$$
$$38 \quad = \quad (3 \times 12) \quad + \quad 2$$

From The Algebra Project Inc. Transition Curriculum, Unit 2, Lesson 5, p. 68; with permission.

Next Lynne directs the students to look at the recording sheets for the Winding Game (see Figure 4.5) and gives them an example of how they will fill it out when they play the game. For example, "If Jasmine is the first member of the team to play, you write her name on the first space under "Winder." Now let's establish the order of the teams." There are four teams in the room, so Lynne assigns each a spot on the practice sheet signifying the order in which they will play the game. When students watch the players complete their trips around the circle, they write the number of winds in the "W" column on the sheet, the residue or remainder number in its column, and the equation in division form A in the corresponding space on the practice sheet. Students can also write the Zodiac sign in the column designated for it.

FIGURE 4.5 RECORDING CHART FOR THE WINDING GAME

Team Name	W	Residue	Zodiac Sign	Your Equation Based on Your Observation
Winder				
Winder				
Winder				
Winder				

From The Algebra Project Inc. Transition Curriculum, Unit 2, Lesson 5, p. 70; with permission.

Clarifying with an example, Lynne asks the students what would be the wind if the number were 26. Several students respond, "2"; others reply, "I still don't get it." Lynne directs the students to decide within their groups who will go first, second, and so on. Sensing that some students are a bit confused, Lynne tells the class, "This is just a practice game; it is not for points. Although we will be playing games for points during this term, this game isn't one of those kinds. You will be able to ask your team for help in figuring out the wind number, the equation, and so forth. You will get clearer about this as it goes along. And one other thing—one sheet that will help you is the sheet of equivalence classes that you made out in your groups earlier. If, for example, Marcus happens to pull the number 42, you can tell by looking at the sheet that he's going to wind 3 times and that he'll sit on chair 6, right?"

> *Lynne:* OK, Marcus, I guess you're first. Pick a number from the envelope. Everybody needs to be very quiet while Marcus is doing this so you can really concentrate. Now, what's the one you always start at?

> *Students:* The monkey.

Marcus draws a number and backs away from the group so he can read the number in private. He walks up to the monkey chair and announces to the class, "I'm starting." Marcus walks around the circle six times and drops into the buffalo chair.

> *Lynne:* Let's see what we have. What was Marcus' wind? Tymesha?

> *Tymesha:* Six.

> *Lynne:* The residue?

> *Diego:* Five.

Lynne: And what Zodiac sign is that? Anthony?

Anthony: The buffalo.

Lynne: Now let's hear the equation. We need it in division form A, remember.

Stasha: That would be $77 = 6 \times 12 + 5$.

Lynne: If you didn't get that equation, write it in now. Your turn will come tomorrow. Let me leave you with this: the way I wound is not the only way to wind around the circle. With more practice you might find more efficient ways to wind around the circle.

As the students are putting away their notebooks and getting ready to leave Lynne's class for the day, Nathan is overheard saying, "I know another fun way." Michelle inquires, "What is your way?" "To get 77, I'd go around 10 times, then go backward 4 times, then figure out how many chairs to walk— like 5 chairs—so I'd end up at the right one. That would really confuse the class! But I think I'd be right!" declares Nathan grinning.

Yvelyne's visit to Lynne's class at Young Achievers comes to an end, but not before several students wave a happy farewell to her as they exit the classroom. "Come back to see us, Dr. McCarthy." A little stunned, she replies, "Thanks for making me part of your class. I'd love to come back." And as I turn off the tape, I find myself saying, "I'd love to visit, too."

DISCUSSION BETWEEN COLLEAGUES

What is your philosophy of teaching mathematics?

> Learning math happens best when the students and teachers are working as a community. The focus of the students in the math class should not be just on the teacher, but on each other as co-learners. Constructing mathematics knowledge is a social event. Each student's voice is important; each has something to contribute.

So how do you go about creating a community in your classroom?

> It takes a lot of patience and time up front. One of the first things I do at the beginning of the school year is to have discussions with the class. We establish the procedures, the atmosphere that allows each student to do his/her best work. We post the results of the discussions. It is my job as the teacher to hold the class to carry out what we have agreed on. Sometimes I use a contract approach that we revisit throughout the year. The contract spells out what each student contributes and what the students expect from each other. There is another important point: I do not send anyone away from the class—ever!

YA has a support team that deals with disruptive students, but I do not have to use the team. I create a place where students want to be and not leave.

How do your students handle the community approach?

Students are very conscious of the community. The students monitor each other's responses to the priorities of the class. They are aware that everybody brings something to the table. There is no feeling that there are two camps in the room—those who can and those who can't. Both boys and girls get equal chances, too. So, if you are calling only on boys one day, the students will let you know!

How do you get the students to work together to form a team?

Early in the school year we have a discussion about the roles and responsibilities of working as a team. We establish five roles: facilitator, timekeeper, materials manager, recorder, and reporter. We cycle the roles so that each student gets a chance to do each one. There is some flexibility in carrying out the roles. For example, the team gets a chance to decide how to record the data, how to report their findings, and so forth. And there is individual work, too. After working on some task individually, a student brings it back to the team.

Your school's philosophy maintains that the school has a culturally relevant curriculum. What is it that you do that makes the Algebra Project culturally relevant?

Even though I use the connected math curriculum (CMP curriculum), it is the Algebra Project curriculum process that makes the curriculum culturally relevant for children; it is children's culture versus some curriculum developer's culture. There are instances in the CMP curriculum when some of the contexts are not relevant to the children here, so we have to substitute a context that is more relevant to our students. One of things students do in the "Data about Us" CMP unit is to figure out different kinds of averages. Instead of using the data given in the book, they generate their own data. They collect their own data about how long it takes different people in the classroom to get to school, how far away from school they live, how that might affect the time that people arrive at school, and so forth. It is their data rather than the book's data. Sometimes we compare that data with the data in their books, but it is really that Algebra Project push that says, "Find the experience that students have, so that they all have a place to enter in." The students all bring something to the table, whether it is an experience they had before or one that they are creating new. While generating their data and constructing their understanding, they have a place to write things down and revise. They refine their ideas and make changes as their understandings clarify. I urge them not to erase. I usually say, "Write your new thinking." The student's voice is so important. And once students hear themselves voicing their ideas in the class, they are never the same afterwards.

Why focus on Asian culture to teach African Americans?

Do you know where that focus came from? When Bob (Moses) designed the curriculum, he wanted a link to the social studies unit on China that his students were learning. But, you know, it is a common experience for students to go to Chinese restaurants. The Chinatown of our city is culturally connected to other parts of the city. Our students have taken field trips there. Occasionally, you have to adjust the zodiac-focus because of religious reasons, but then you just use another cycle to help develop the concepts.

Would you teach that lesson differently if you had a different group of students. Let's say they were all Euro-Americans, all white kids. Would it be different?

The conversation might be different.

So, in essence, what you are saying is that the lesson is such that it does not matter what kind of students you have as long as you are doing good teaching.

It is a lesson that I have done in a predominantly white class, and what counts the most are the experiences the kids are bringing to the table. I may use different strategies with different classes: for example, more individual work versus more work in teams. It really varies from class to class. In general, the Algebra Project is meant for any group of people who do not feel confident as math learners. That was Bob Moses' deliberate intention—to put a floor under the students he worked with. The curriculum empowers those students whose voices are not heard in the math class to be mathematically powerful people. Even in an all-white class, there are some whose voices are not heard. This may be especially true of middle school girls for whom the curriculum makes a big difference. It is very powerful!

Is there any teaching method you can consistently apply based on the culture of your students? If you looking at African American students, are there some overriding teaching patterns that you see?

My teaching practices or style of teaching is pretty consistent regardless of the population, I think. It is not different because of the racial make-up of the class.

How do you assess the students' learning?

> In the Algebra Project curriculum there are no formal tests. Homework is a big part of the assessment. Getting the students to do homework is not an issue. Each student's attitude is, "I'm responsible; I can't let my team down." At the beginning of the year the students and I develop a 0- to 4-point rubric for assessing their work. I find that having a rubric helps students know how to interpret a score of "3" so much better than just guessing. In the CMP program there are end-of-the-unit projects, quizzes, and unit tests.

You also have a state-mandated test, right?

> Yes, we have the MCAT. I do not stop the regular lessons to teach to the test. I know it is a real struggle for teachers not to use class time to prepare for just one test. What I have found from using the Algebra Project curriculum is that it establishes for kids that math is a human endeavor. They can do math! Their efficacy as mathematicians is tremendous, so when they approach new things or meet a question they are not sure about on the MCAT, they have not lost confidence and work to figure it out.

What supports does your school have to help teachers be successful?

> YA respects the need of teachers for time: time to interact with each other, to problem-solve around the kids, and to work with curriculum. Teachers have two–three hours per week for team meetings; they have grade-level meetings twice a week; and, on Fridays, the students are dismissed at noon so the upper school and lower school staff can meet all afternoon. There are lots of support people here, too. And we seek a lot of parental involvement. For example, before beginning a new unit of instruction, teachers send a letter home informing the parents and giving them suggestions for helping their children.

Do you think that being of the same race as most of the students somehow empowers you to make some connection that may not have happened if you had a class of white students?

> Yes, and no. Here my being an African American woman does give me certain leverage over maybe another teacher who is not an African American.

Do you think that leverage is that they respect you because, "she's knows what she's talking about; she has a sense of us as students; she knows where we are coming from?"

Not necessarily. I do not send my students out of my classes. Most of the time, when they are asked to leave, it is by the white teachers. I taught in a mostly-white school and did not send students out of my class to the principal either. It really depends on your expectations of yourself as a teacher.

But, Lynne, you are middle class; you do not look black; and I could not tell over the phone if you are black or white. Do you consider yourself African American?

Oh, yes. It's interesting. When I first came here, I was told by a staff member: "You are not from here; you will not know how to teach our students."

So how did you react to this comment? And what did you do?

I was angry at the comment and said to myself, "We'll see." I just did what I came to do. When things did not work, I said to myself, "Maybe they are right." But I knew I was in the right place and at the right time. I believe in what the Algebra Project represents and who it is for. And I knew what was behind the comment. The principal likes to hire from the community because those outside do not know the struggles. So I kept coming back every day. Eventually, someone told me the other teachers were all asking, "When are the students going to make her cry?"

What recommendation would you make to a teacher who is about to begin teaching in your school?

I would highly recommend that they sit in on many classes here.

Why is that? Do you think they will find things that are different from many other classes? Let's say they were teachers who have been teaching already. What would they see here that is so different that you think they really need to see it in order to succeed?

I think they would see how much the teacher needs to establish a community in the classroom. I think they would get a better sense of what it is that children bring with them to school and how different teachers throughout the school tap into the little strengths and work from that place. I think people often come here who really want to teach at Young Achievers, and they have this ideal picture in their heads of what they are going to teach in the inner city and how they will make a huge difference. Then, when people actually come, it is a shock, and they feel completely thrown out of the water. It is hard for some teachers to hold on to their beliefs and ideals of what kids can do. They question whether students can master algebra by the end of the eighth grade, for example. Teachers have to figure out what makes the students tick; they have to figure out what makes themselves tick. Teachers have to look at themselves and their own practices; this is not easy for some people. During their first year here, they will know if they will make it here. But once they figure out how it all works, they will be successful—and very rewarded.

COMMENTARY

Secondary math teacher, Robert Moses, taught mathematics to his children at home to supplement the mathematics they had in school. In 1982, his daughter's teacher invited Moses to work with students on algebra in the eighth grade classroom in the Open Program at Martin Luther King School in Cambridge, MA. He continued his work the following year when his son entered seventh grade. The group studying algebra grew, but still focused on academically talented students. Academically talented African American males, in particular, felt uncomfortable joining the group because they would be separated from their friends who were on other math tracks. As a parent-organizer, Moses, decided to take action. He drew on his background as a civil rights organizer in Mississippi in the 1960s to make the learning of algebra more than a curriculum issue; it became a broader political issue. He began a dialogue with parents, teachers, and administrators in the Open Program. Eventually, consensus was reached that each student in the Open Program could achieve math literacy.

The results of this change in philosophy included changes in the content and methods of teaching math, classroom involvement of parents and their participation in workshops on student achievement and self-esteem, emphasis on students' self-motivation to succeed, the recruitment of African American college graduates to serve as role models and tutors, and the birth of the Algebra Project (Moses et al. 1989). As Kamii (1990) points out, "The Project was not designed as an elaborate intervention grounded on a systemic examination of issues raised in the research literatures of mathematics education or psychology. Instead, its frame of reference was responding to problems as they arose in the context of students' efforts to learn algebra and seizing opportunities for experimentation with classroom activities and teaching formats as they presented themselves each day" (395).

As a philosophy, the Algebra Project contributes to mathematics and science literacy, which is a prerequisite for employment and citizenship. Three broad goals are addressed: to develop mathematically literate and motivated students who will master the college preparatory mathematics necessary for careers in which they will need mathematics; to produce teachers who create learning environments in which students connect real-life experiences to their construction of mathematics knowledge; and to build a community of nurturing support for students.

As a curriculum, the Algebra Project Transition Curriculum follows a five-step curricular process. First, the program uses physical events from students' everyday experiences that are the links between the physical world and the abstractions of mathematics. Next, students make a pictorial representation/model of physical events. Then, students use their own intuitive language to talk/write about the events. Next, the teacher uses regimented English sentences to lead students from their intuitive language responses into equations to represent the physical events. Last, students begin by developing their own symbols and then are introduced to standard symbols (Silva et al. 1990).

The experiential learning of the Algebra Project Transition Curriculum helps students to create the conceptual language of mathematics, honors how students think and their experiences, emphasizes group work and cooperation, and assists students to clarify and organize their thinking as they present their math understanding to their peers (Checkley and Moses 2001). The Algebra Project emphasizes efficacy and the belief that confidence and effective effort are alternatives to an ability model of learning (Moses et al. 1989). Confidence is a strong predictor of mathematical course taking and has a significant, positive correlation with mathematics achievement (Reyes 1984).

Lynne is not only an exemplary teacher, but also a developer and a champion of the Algebra Project in the Cambridge area. The lesson profiled in this chapter exemplifies the philosophy and pedagogy of the Algebra Project in several ways. The lesson connects to the students' real-world experience of the Chinese Zodiac. In it there are multiple opportunities for the students to articulate their understanding through both action and language. In the group setting, students acting as a community of learners negotiate mathematical meaning. The lesson uses games to establish patterns and rules.

What can educators who are not teaching the Algebra Project's Transition Curriculum learn from Lynne's approach? Does her approach address what experts suggest are effective approaches for teaching mathematics to African American learners? Wiest (2001) points out that "many strategies suggested for diverse learners merely reflect what we believe to be good teaching" (21). She stresses the impact of questioning strategies as both cognitive and affective learning strategies. Lynne's questions invite her students to think deeply about both their own and their peers' understanding. White (2000) cautions that it is not enough to ask challenging questions and to listen to students' answers. Instruction must be adjusted according to the teacher's interpretation of the students' responses. She adds, "All students, and African American students in particular, need opportunities to solve problems on their own and share their solutions with peers and teachers" (31).

Like the students in Lynne's class, the subjects in a study by Malloy and Jones (1998) of African American students' problem-solving development frequently used holistic reasoning approaches and displayed much confidence in their ability to solve the problems even when they were not successful. The Algebra Project's (and Lynne's) approaches to problem solving (situations relevant to her students' interests, student-directed discussions, real-life activities, multi-solution problems) preserve the students' self-efficacy and build a firm foundation for their future success in algebra. These approaches align with the recommendations of Smith, Stiff, and Petree (2000), who report that with the least academically prepared students, "open-ended problems rooted in concrete, real-life settings worked best" (92).

Lynne employs what Ladson-Billings (1998) calls "culturally relevant pedagogy" in her math class. According to Ladson-Billings the hallmarks of culturally relevant pedagogy include student-posed and teacher-posed problems; students treated as competent; high expectations set by the teacher; use of prior knowledge as a bridge to new learning; the extension of students' thinking beyond what they already know; and strong interpersonal relationships of teachers with students. In accordance with the Equity Principle of NCTM's *Principles and Standards for School Mathematics* (2000), Lynne communicates high expectations for her students. According to Rowser and Koontz (1995), "The effectiveness of the teacher in motivating and involving students in the learning process . . . and the communication . . . of the teacher in manifesting his or her attitudes, beliefs, and expectations for student achievement determine the quality of the academic experience" (452). Walker and McCoy (1997) emphasize the link between the teacher's personal interaction with the students and their desire to perform well in the class. Mathematically successful students in their study reported that the positive encouragement given to them by teachers and parents helped them to realize the importance of mathematics and motivated them to take more mathematics courses. Walker and McCoy caution that the teacher of mathematics "must realize that his or her classroom environment may be damaging to the confidence of African American students" (79).

In summary, African American students will be well served in the mathematics class if their teachers, like Lynne, keep in mind the suggestions of Ladson-Billings (1998). Students who are treated as competent are likely to demonstrate competence. The provision of instructional scaffolding for students allows them to move from what they know to what they do not know. In fact, the major focus of the classroom must be instructional (no busy work). Because real education is about extending students' thinking and abilities beyond what they already know, teachers should present challenging content. Finally, effective pedagogical practice involves in-depth knowledge of students as well as subject matter.

CONTACT

Lynne Godfrey
Young Achievers Science and Mathematics Pilot School
25 Walk Hill St.
Jamaica Plain, MA 02130
Phone: 617-635-6804
E-mail: YoungAchievers@Boston.k12.ma.us
Website: http://boston.k12.ma.us/schools

UNIT OVERVIEW:
THE CHINESE ZODIAC AND THE
DIVISION ALGORITHM

Aim: How can the Chinese Zodiac help us to examine important relationships in the division of numbers?

Objectives: Students build on their intuitive understanding of equivalence in everyday situations and apply that practical knowledge to exploring the cycles and equivalence classes within the Chinese Zodiac. Students move from the physical event of winding around chairs to employing a formula or general rule for finding the zodiac sign for any year: Year = 12 × number of Winds + Remainder. In the form for the division algorithm, this becomes $d = nq + r$, where d is the dividend, n is a whole number, q is the quotient, and r is the remainder.

Grade Level: Sixth grade

Number of 60-Minute Periods: Two periods for this lesson; 12–15 days for the whole unit.

Source: Algebra Project Transition Curriculum

Mathematics Principles and Standards Addressed:

♦ Principles for equity, curriculum, teaching, learning, assessment

♦ Mathematics as problem solving, communication, connection, and representation

♦ Algebra: Understand patterns, relations, and functions; represent and analyze mathematical situations and structures.

♦ Number and operations: Understand meanings of operations and how they relate to one another.

Prerequisites:

♦ Previous experience with equivalence, equality, and "making-do"

♦ Knowledge of the Chinese Zodiac

Mathematical Concepts:

♦ Equivalence and division/multiplication relationships

♦ Division algorithm

Materials and Tools:

♦ Place mat of the Chinese Zodiac

♦ Drawing paper and art supplies

♦ Worksheets from the Algebra Project Transition Curriculum (see figures in this lesson)

♦ Twelve chairs arranged in a circle

Management Procedures:

♦ Arrange twelve chairs in a circle for the Winding Game portion of the lesson.

♦ Divide students into groups for the purpose of designing the Zodiac sign posters, to complete the equivalence charts, and to play the Winding Game.

Assessment: The completed worksheets become part of each student's portfolio compiled throughout the Algebra Project units. There is no formal test covering these topics. The primary goal of the Algebra Project units is to strengthen the confidence of the students in their study of mathematics.

5

GEORGINE ROLDAN: HISPANICS AND HEALTH ISSUES

My school is located in a primarily Black, impoverished neighborhood with a large population of Hispanics. There are a lot of drugs in the neighborhood, and many children are drug babies. Our student mobility rate, which is nearly 50%, is caused primarily by many parents seeking schools in better neighborhoods and by other parents taking advantage of Florida's voucher system. My fourth grade English Speakers of Other Languages (ESOL) students are from different countries and from low socioeconomic backgrounds. They need a caring environment to help them adjust. Some of them speak more English than others, but of 16 students, only two speak English well enough to understand what's going on. In this lesson on making bar graphs to represent favorite foods, my students show how well they can work together to communicate their mathematical understanding. Simultaneously, I try to increase their awareness of diabetes, a disease that disproportionately attacks Latinos, Blacks, and Native Americans.

Georgine Roldan, Fourth grade teacher
Frederick Douglass Elementary School, Miami, FL

Georgine Roldan submitted a videotaped lesson for this book months before I (Yvelyne, first author) could find the time to visit her and her students. Thus, the goal for my visit would not be to see her lesson in progress, but to get a richer sense of the teacher-to-student interactions that I viewed on the tape. I thought that Mardi Gras time in New Orleans would be perfect. To my disappointment, she said it would not be an ideal time because they would be undergoing Florida's high stakes test called the Florida Comprehensive Assessment Test (FCAT). To heighten the anxiety level, her school was already labeled a "double-F" because in two out of the past four years, its FCAT ratings

51

were Fs (Ds on the other two). However, visiting on the last day would be fine since testing sessions were over by lunchtime, and she would probably have students watch a math video in the afternoon.

As I drove to the school, I thought about its demographics and students. "Our children have a lot of issues," Georgine had said. Indeed, Frederick Douglass is situated in a Black community and is largely composed of Latino (60%) and African Americans students (33%), with 99% of the students receiving free or reduced lunches and living in low-income neighborhoods. The students walk from neighboring housing projects or are bussed from Little Havana, an impoverished Latino section of the city. Due to the high mobility rate, the school's previous year's population of 700 students was down to 635, a number which would have been lower had it not been for the arrival of new immigrant students. Georgine's ESOL students are recent immigrants from Central and South America, with only two students commanding enough English to read a complete sentence. They are self-contained with Georgine as both their ESOL and regular teacher.

As I looked outside the school, I noticed students standing in line in a well-kept basketball court. Teachers chatted easily and congenially with students in English or Caribbean-accented English, or Spanish, as they shared encouraging words about the ensuing test. Entering the school, the president of the PTA was supervising the sale of small items for a fundraiser while simultaneously greeting other parents who had come to serve as volunteers for any testing duties. Georgine introduced me to her principal, Ms. McGinnis, who was dressed in jeans because she had promised a fifth grade class that she would jog around the court with them after their exam. "Georgine is an excellent teacher," she said, "one of the best in the school. Her students performed very well on the previous FCAT." I nodded in agreement as Georgine introduced me to Susana Bello, a fifth grade mathematics teacher who would later be joining us for discussion of the profile questions.

While Georgine's second-floor classroom was bare of decorations because of the test, the first floor hallway near the entrance was decorated with both posters and students' work celebrating Black History month. Other posters written in English, Spanish, and Haitian Creole declared that reading was a fun and good habit. This was not a crumbling school packed with teachers of low morale and students running wild. It appeared that the principal, teachers, parents, and school ambiance projected a positive and supportive environment for this diverse student population—the students appeared to know and appreciate that.

My thoughts then turned to a host of questions: So what's not working here? Why a double-F, and what were the consequences of being double F? What were the implications to the school from the *No Child Left Behind Act* (NCLB) and the Florida school choice system? How does Georgine address the needs of reform mandates and, more critically, those of her students in her day-to-day teaching and student interactions? I knew that answers to these questions and others would have to wait until the afternoon after the exam. It was now only early morning, so I quieted my thoughts by rereading Georgine's unit in which she launches an investigation leading to data analysis and awareness of diabetes by appealing to students' shared appreciation for Latino food.

DAY 1: ENGAGING STUDENTS

Georgine begins the lesson by reading the poem, "Nature Knows Its Math" (Graham 1997). After every line she reads in English, she has the class repeat it. Although she reads the poem in English, she uses Spanish whenever necessary to help students understand and to explain the mathematical terms.

Moving on to the day's lesson, Georgine tells the students, "Today we will review a type of graph using bars. How many of you remember making bar graphs last year?" (A few hands are raised.) "Well, we will refresh memories and see how much you remember as we create such graphs to shed light on important health information."

Georgine tells the students to take out the homework requiring a tally of the number of family members' or friends' preferences for three different Taco Bell foods: tacos, chalupas, and burritos. "There were two questions I wanted you to answer as part of your homework. The first one was which one of the three foods they like best, and the second was which of the foods do you think is the healthiest. Georgine then elicits the results for the first question:

Georgine: Allan, tell us where you are from and how many people liked tacos in your house?"

Allan: I am from Honduras, and we all preferred tacos—ten of us.

Georgine: How many of you are from Honduras? (*Six students raise their hands.*) Did most of your relatives prefer tacos too? (*The students nod in agreement.*) Lionel, where are you from, and what were your results?

Lionel: I am from Argentina, and my family liked burritos.

Jeffrey: In Puerto Rico they eat all three, so my house had some people for each.

Georgine: Now I'd like all of you to give me your results so that we can keep a tally on the overhead project.

After getting the tallies, Georgine tells students to record the totals because the homework will be to compare the responses with a bar graph.

GROUP WORK

The students are already seated in groups of four or five. She tells the students to work within their groups to compile and display the group's data with a bar graph. She adds, "You must also calculate the mean, mode, and median for each food, and then draw a bar graph to represent your group's data. Pick a recorder who will record the tallies, a captain who will represent the data with a bar graph, and a reporter who will share the results with the rest of the class." Using rulers, pencils, and construction paper, the students proceed to do the task. They start discussing different ideas for making their graphs.

Group 1

Jose: We have to make the graph go like this—put the food on one line and the numbers on the other line. I want to be team captain. I don't see the construction paper. Where is it?

Mirna: I think the construction paper is under the poem sheet—here it is. We already did the tallies for our group. But I want to be team captain too.

Jose: Go ahead Mirna. You be captain since you found the paper.

Mirna: No, it's ok. You can do it.

Jose eagerly accepts the role and picks up the ruler to begin creating the axis for the graph.

Group 2

Jessica: See, these are the numbers, but how should we put them on paper?

William: I think we have to do a straight line to form the graph.

Pablo: We have to use a ruler, but how far up should we go to draw the line?

William: Well, let's see. How many tacos do we have?

Pablo: Three.

William: No. I mean, how many altogether from the three of us?

Barry: Oh. I don't have that count, so we have to do that first. How many did you get for tacos, Jessica?

Group 3

Sandra: OK. I will be the Captain. Let's get the numbers each of you got for your family.

Juan: I will add them up. (*He goes around and looks at each person's data.*) OK. I got that seventeen people liked tacos altogether.

Sandra: And how many chalupas?

Juan: We have 17 tacos and eight burritos and two chalupas.

Sandra: Now how high should it go? (*Miguel and Carlos place their hands over the grid paper that she is working on to show how high a bar should be.*)

Group 4

Roberto: OK. Now, how can we know how high to go?

Mario: How many tacos did we get?

Kelvin: We got 12 but does that tell you that it should be higher than 12?

Hector: I know how to do it! (*He takes the ruler as Mario grabs it back.*)

Mario: No. I can do it. Let's just go up to the highest number. How do you spell "number"?

Anna: I think it's *n-u-m-e-r*.

Group 2

Jessica: Tacos got the highest number of 23. Should we just start from zero and go up to 25?

Allan: No. It looks like going by fives would be better. Let's go by fives, like 5, 10, 15, 20, and 25.

William: We can do that. I will get the mean and Barry, you get the median.

After some time Georgine asks each group captain to share the results of the group. The graphs show students using scales counting consecutively from 1 to 20, or 1 to 15, and by fives (see Figure 5.1). Georgine goes around the groups and assigns each group relevant math questions about the graphs. She concludes the lesson by saying, "For homework, you have three things to do: Make a bar graph of the results for the whole class and make up three math questions that you can answer from the graphs. Next, think about the important elements that make up a good bar graph because tomorrow we will develop a rubric for assessing each of them. Finally, be prepared to share thoughts about foods you think are healthy." She collects the graphs and dismisses the class.

DAY 2: ASSESSMENT

Georgine begins the next day with a quick review of the graphing lesson by asking the class for a summary.

Jose: Yesterday, we made a graph to count how many people liked different kinds of food from Taco Bell.

Georgine: Very good. What we are going to do today is to come to agreement on the elements of a good bar graph so that we can assess each other's graphs. I'm going to ask each table to share something you need to have on your graph. Let's begin with Maria's table.

FIGURE 5.1   STUDENT'S SAMPLE WORK FOR BAR GRAPH

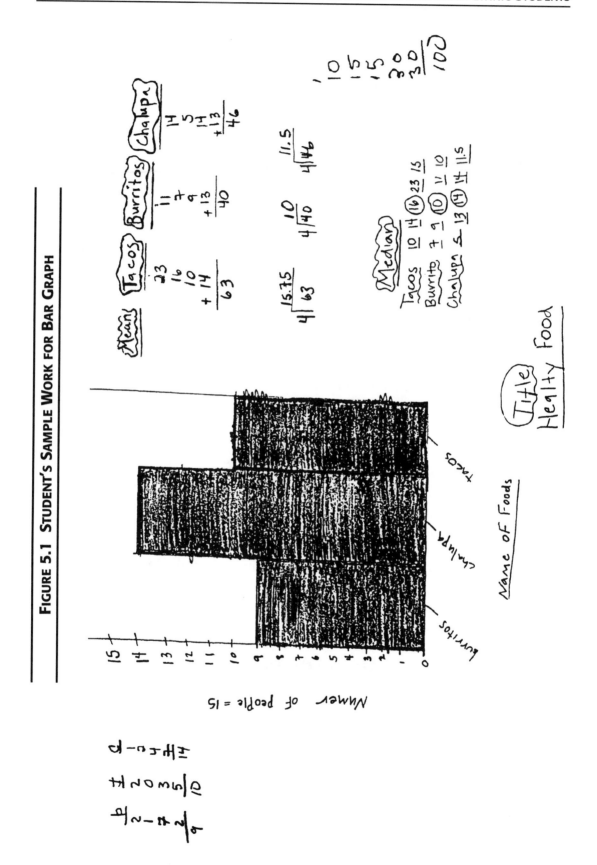

Maria: Well, they have to show numbers and types of food.

Sara: The names of the food—They should go on the bottom.

Georgine: Bottom of what?

Sara: They go on the bottom of the line.

Georgine: How many lines does the graph have?

Mario: Two.

Georgine: Two lines, like this? *(She draws two nonperpendicular intersecting lines.)*

Roberto: No. One has to be vertical, and the other one is horizontal.

Juan: When we do the graph, we should use a ruler to measure and to keep it neat.

Mario: We need a title too.

Georgine: Now we have to decide on total points. How many points should all the parts add up to?

Mirna: Let's go up to 100 points.

Jose: Let horizontal line with label get 15 points.

Roberto: Vertical line, 15 points, too.

Georgine: Suppose a student makes the lines but forgets to label. What will you do?

Mary: Take away five points and give only 10 points.

Sandra: The title should be about 10 points.

Jessica: Then give 10 points each for getting the mean, median and mode, so that's 30 points there.

Georgine: What else do we need?

Melvin: The bar graphs. We got 30 points left, so make each of them 10 points.

Georgine: Ok. Now I am going to give each group the graph of a different group to grade. I want you to decide with your group the number of elements that are present and to then compute the grade for the graph. Refer to your rubric on the board. *(Georgine writes,)*

RUBRIC:

   ♦ 10 points each for the bar graphs (30 points total)

   ♦ 10 points each for mean, median and mode (30 points total)

   ♦ 15 points each for horizontal and vertical line with labels (30 points total)

   ♦ 10 points for the title

Students gather around the graph papers and can be heard making comments such as, "Let's check to see that they have all the parts"; "Oh no. They left out the title"; "Check to see if they calculated the median right."

Georgine: Please return your graph to the appropriate group. I will not put these grades in my grade book, but I will do so for tonight's homework. Here is what you have to do: You have already completed the graphs for the whole class's data for today's homework. How many of you would have gotten 100%? (*No one raises a hand.*) What I want you to do tonight is to review that graph and to be sure that all of the elements that we decided are important are present. Tomorrow we will grade each other's papers for a related problem, and I will enter the grade in my book. You should all get 100% this time, right? (*Students nod.*)

DAY 3: HEALTHY FOODS LESSON

"Now, let's turn our attention to healthy foods. When was the last time we talked about healthy foods in this class?" William replies, "In class, when we learned about the Food Pyramid." She asks the class to share which of the Taco Bell foods they think is the healthiest. Some students' responses include "Tacos because they have a lot of different foods from the food pyramid"; "Chalupas because they have a lot of vegetables"; "Burritos because they have a lot of meat." Georgine then says, "When we talk about what is healthy for you, it is relative to your physical condition and how often you eat that particular food. Some people, for example, shouldn't have too much salt in their diet because it causes their knees to swell. Diabetes is another example of a disease that requires careful attention to diet. What is diabetes?"

Franco: Diabetes is a sickness that makes people can't eat sugar.

Georgine: Good, Franco. And it's also a disease that has no cure and affects more Latin Americans than any other group in the USA.

Carmen: Blacks get it too, Mrs. Roldan, because my grandfather has it, and whenever Grandma makes cake she always says, "And none for you mister!" (*Students laugh.*)

Georgine: I'm glad you added that Carmen. Blacks, Latinos, and Native Americans are the groups most affected by diabetes. So you are also saying that sugar is a problem for persons with diabetes. But is it only sugar? Remember when we talked about the Food Pyramid, we talked about not having too much of certain types of food so as to avoid getting too fat for our age. Too much sugar could cause that, but what else do we eat that gets turned into sugar?

Tiana: You mean like foods with lots of bread?

Georgine: Yes. Foods with carbohydrates produce sugars in our system, and the more of them we eat, the greater the risk of diabetes. Too much fat is also a danger. My cousin died from diabetes when she was only 35.

Miguel: How did she die?

Georgine: She had kidney problems and then a heart attack. She had diabetes as a teenager, and she was not careful about taking care of it as she grew older, and that caused her to have other problems.

Carmen: I hope that doesn't happen to my granddaddy.

Georgine: It probably won't happen to him since you're grandma is looking out for him. But let's see what we have to look out for so as to protect our family and ourselves. I have some facts about diabetes that I would like you to read now, and later with your family. Barry, please start reading (see Figure 5.2).

FIGURE 5.2 DIABETES AND FAT AND CHOLESTEROL IN FOODS

Homework: Read this information and share it with your family and friends:

A large number of Latinos, African Americans, and Native Americans have a high rate of diabetes. Diabetes is a deadly disease that affects over 10% of the Latino population. Latinos get this disease twice as many times as the general population. This disease affects the body's ability to process sugar in the way that gives us the amount of energy we need to function. When the sugar in the blood is not regulated, some bad things that could happen to us are that we can become blind, lose a leg, get kidney disease, or have a heart attack and die. There is no cure for diabetes. A real and dangerous fact about this disease is that we could have it and not know it. Doctors think it is hereditary. It is called the silent killer because it may not show up before we become adults.

There is no cure for diabetes, so you have to carefully monitor your diet if you have it. One way to prevent diabetes is to get tested regularly by a doctor. Other important ways are to exercise and avoid getting too fat for your age or height. So, if you are overweight and there are people in your family who have diabetes, please get checked by a doctor! Watching our diet by not eating too much food with lost of fat or high cholesterol levels is very important.

Barry reads the passage with frequent supportive corrections from Georgine and students. She then distributes Taco Bell nutrition guides which she had ordered from Taco Bell (1-800-TACOBELL) and tells the students to study the nutrients listed for each of the foods.

Georgine: There are lots of nutrients listed, but let us focus only on the fat and cholesterol levels which contribute to diabetes. Eating 2000 calories per day is used as a standard for determining the numbers on this chart. Some people may need a little more or fewer calories depending on age and weight. Look at the chart. Suppose you want to be careful about how much fat and cholesterol you eat today. Which of the Tacos would you need to look out for?

Maria: The last one in the Tacos column has more fat, but the Soft Chicken Supreme has more cholesterol.

Georgine: Can all of you read the table? Maria, come show the class how you got your answer from my overhead copy.

Maria uses her finger to trace down the fat and cholesterol columns as she explains her answer.

Georgine: Another important number on the Taco Bell nutrition guide is the Percent Daily Value. Who can tell us what the number means? (*Students are silent.*) Remember that if we start with 100% as the amount of a nutrient to eat daily, then the percent value tells us what percent of a nutrient we get by eating that food. How many grams of fat are in the Chicken Supreme, and what is the percent daily value for that amount?

Melvin: It's 5 grams and has a 25% daily value.

Georgine: Now, let's look at the grilled steak burrito. If you were taking precautions against getting diabetes, should you eat three in one day?

Enrique: That is too much fat. That would give you three times 45%, and that is way more than 100%.

Mirna: Next to the Percent Daily Value, they have something called the diabetic exchange. What does that mean?

Georgine: People with diabetes have to carefully monitor what they eat. The diabetic exchange system lists exchanges they can make for certain foods. For example, let's say that they can have 2000 calories and want to eat tacos. One taco can be exchanged for the meat and fat limitation. The one-half under starch and bread means that one taco substitutes for the starch or for ½ slice of bread. Do you see how difficult it can be to have diabetes? You must protect yourself by having your family bring you to the doctor for regular check-ups in addition to eating well and exercising. Now let's return to the question: Which of the foods would be the healthiest if we were concerned about lowering our fat and cholesterol intake? To answer this question, we will complete the table in the second handout I will give you" (see Figure 5.3). For homework, I want you to share the diabetes information with your family. I will also give you a translation of the information in Spanish to read with your parents and friends. Right now, complete questions 1–3 in your group, and do questions 4 and 5 for homework.

FIGURE 5.3 FOOD VALUE CHART

EXERCISE. From the Taco Bell chart:

List the name of the highest fat and cholesterol content food for each category.

Enter the numbers required in the table for that food. (*Readers:* Answers are given in the table in parentheses.)

Answer the questions that follow the chart.

Food	*Fat* (grams)	*% Fat Value*	*Cholesterol* (grams)	*% Cholesterol Value*
Taco- Highest Fat Name: (DD Supreme)	(18)	(28)	(35)	(12)
Taco- Highest cholesterol Name: (Chick Supreme)	(11)	(17)	(45)	(15)
Chalupa- Highest fat Name: (Baja beef)	(29)	(45)	(30)	(10)
Chalupa- Highest fat Name: (Nacho beef)	(24)	(37)	(27)	(9)
Burrito- Highest fat Name: (Grilled beef)	(35)	(54)	(55)	(18)
Burrito- Highest cholesterol Name: (Grilled chicken)	(28)	(43)	(70)	(23)
Homework: Your favorite: Name:				

1. From the table, which two foods have the highest fat and cholesterol content?

2. If you were to have foods from this table for lunch and dinner on the same day, which two would you choose and why?

FIGURE 5.3 FOOD VALUE CHART *(CONTINUED)*

3. Does the table mean that Taco Bell foods are not healthy? Explain.

4. For homework, complete the last row in the table for you favorite Taco Bell meal. Next, look at the Taco Bell chart and list some of the other nutrients found in your meal. Is that a healthy meal for you? Explain.

5. Find two friends who are in the sixth grade and share the diabetes information with them. Ask them and family members to help you answer these next questions:

   a. If there are 12 million Latinos in the U.S., approximately how many may have diabetes?

   b. There are 17 Latinos in this class and 13 in Ms. Bello's class. What is the expected number from both classes who may get diabetes?

   c. What can you do to protect yourself, family, and friends from this disease?

Georgine circulates around the room as students study the chart to complete the assignment. She hears Jose say, "Wow. Look at the fat in that last burrito on the list—the one with the steak." And Sandra replies, "Look at the cholesterol of the chicken on top of it." Georgine asks students to think about whether the results may imply that Taco Bell foods are unhealthy.

Maria: Maybe.

Carmen: It will depend on how often we eat the food.

Georgine: So varying the diet to include different types of food is helpful. As we learned from the Food Pyramid, we do have to balance what we eat. Exercising and seeing a doctor for regular check ups are a must for keeping us fit.

Maria: I'll bet you a McDonald's hamburger has lots more cholesterol in it.

Georgine: Raise your hands if you believe this to be true. *(The class is undecided.)* If you have a computer at home, go to their website where you will find their nutrition chart. Tomorrow we will use our computers to go there and test some of your ideas about nutrition comparisons between the two.

Georgine writes the site on the board and concludes her lesson (www.mcdonalds.com/countries/usa/food/nutrition_facts/index.html).

DISCUSSION AMONG COLLEAGUES

Both Georgine and Susana participate in the discussion. The first segment focuses on Georgine and her students.

Georgine, what is your philosophy of teaching mathematics?

> Students should be given opportunities to learn important concepts from different learning tools such as technology, the text, and manipulatives. As much as possible, applications that are meaningful to the students should be incorporated in the lessons. I try to present material in various ways so that students have a better chance for understanding.

Are there any teaching practices that you consistently apply based on the culture of your students?

> My students love to work in groups, so my classroom is set up for group work. They also respond well to visuals, hands-on, and repetition of terms.

What would you do differently if you taught this lesson to students of a different culture?

> Because information about diabetes is important to any culture, I would probably not change the content. However, if there was a problem or disease known to affect this different culture, then I would probably do some research to integrate that information into a lesson too. Although I think all students should be given opportunities to work in groups, different students may not need this strategy as often as I provide it for my ESOL students.

How does your being from a similar culture enhance your teaching of the students?

> Being of a similar culture helps because I speak their language and understand their situation. Although my Latin background is Mexican and my students are from different countries, sharing a common language does help to create a bond between us a lot faster. In addition to learning the content, we use Spanish cultural references to gain a deeper understanding of who we are and how we differ, and I always try to stress that what we have in common is greater than the differences.

How do you generally assess students?

> I give my students multiple chances for success. What is most important to me is that they have learned and can apply the important

concepts now—today. I do not hold past, poor test grades against them. Once they grasp the concept, my next focus is helping them to retain it by connecting it to new work as we move forward. I typically give two assessments a week: one is oral and in a group setting; the other is an individual paper and pencil test. They need to be able to succeed on both types of assessments.

How do your students perform in math?

These students do well in math, largely because of a strong foundation in basic skills from their countries. They come already knowing their multiplication tables, unlike many other students in our school. They have a love for mathematics, and I love working with them to sustain it. I also learn from them, too. I was born and educated in America, so I do not compute in the same manner they do. Consider the way they perform subtraction with regrouping. You know what amazes me when they do it? They do not borrow systematically as we do. They do not need to regroup—They just write their answers down, and the answers are always correct. I had one student explain it to me, and I learned that she uses addition to count up all the time instead of subtracting. Rather than borrow, she adds ten to columns in the minuend to count up when necessary and then compensates by adding ten to the subtrahend of the column on the left. She gets her answer much faster than I do with borrowing! It was interesting to then share with her and the rest of the class my algorithm so that we now have two different ways for doing the problem.

Given that you are in a low performing school, what special programs are in place to help all your students succeed?

Georgine: A priority is in building self-esteem so that students feel they can succeed. Our principal is careful to select teachers who are sensitive to our students' needs. As for the academics, we have a before- and after-school tutorial for reinforcements, and that includes working with the computer. Extra curricular activities are also important. For example, we have a big chess club where children come in the mornings to play. We also have tutors come in from community organizations to work one-on-one with those children who show potential to pass the FCAT with a little more help.

Susana: I supervise the chess club, and I am always amazed at the eight to ten students who skip breakfast to show up before class to play. We encourage as much participation as possible because chess demands focused attention and concentration, both of which are requirements for academic success. If our students enjoy the game, then, in my opinion, we should be able to find ways to get them to enjoy learning, too. We were actually spotlighted in the newspaper for our chess team!

Georgine: We are also proud of the music program. Music teachers spend a lot of time with students who can choose to play the flute, violin, or a small xylophone. Students show off their acting, musical, and artistic talents through participation in concerts, plays, and school decorations. We try to showcase their talents at a time when parents can attend. For example, during the Christmas season, the children decorate the building, put on a play, and have a chorus concert in the evenings. The children love these activities, and, of course, the parents enjoy them as well. Parents come and feel proud of the students.

Talk more about parental involvement in the school.

Georgine: Our school has events to attract parents, but unfortunately many of the parents do not attend as much as they should. But I have noticed that in the last two years, we have had a higher number of parents coming. We now want to create a basketball team, and it looks like the parents will agree to help us with it.

Susana: What I think would be a really important thing is for parents to help their children with homework during after-school tutoring. Some parents could attend because they are not working. It's true that there are topics that would be difficult for the parents, but with a supervising teacher, both child and parent could learn together.

How do you feel about FCAT as a measure of your students' competencies?

Georgine: The majority of our students are from low-income households and come to us below grade level, so it really is not fair to measure them against others from more prosperous and richer backgrounds. I think teachers should be accountable for student achievement; however, the basis should start where the students are today, and then growth should be the measurement factor. We get help measuring growth through monthly tests that are required of all students. Our curriculum team specialist does the statistics and then informs us of areas for student improvement. I hate losing students to other schools. Because the ESOL classes had students with fewer than two years of residency, we were left with five out of 23 kids. The others went to different schools based on the school of choice system.

Susana: A good outcome is that the curriculum is coordinated with standards, benchmarks, and grade-level expectations as well as the

FCAT. But the bad thing is that we are given weekly planning forms to follow, and it soon becomes unrealistic to have all students learning the same thing at the same time. Probably the best outcome, however, is that FCAT has many questions focusing on process and problems beyond standard computation. It forces teachers to teach to the test, and, in this case, that is a good thing. If this were not the case, I do not think our students would learn much more beyond the traditional basics.

Georgine: But now consider the ESOL child. An ESOL child who has been in the country for over two years and is still not literate in English, should not be required to pass the FCAT test. The test is all English, and we are not allowed to translate. Furthermore, if at the end of the year this same child fails an ESOL English test that measures English proficiency, he/she is then required to be tested for learning disabilities (LD). Guess what? The LD test is also in English! Why is a child learning disabled because he/she does not know a language? There is no test to accurately measure the ESOL student's cognitive ability; thus, a lot of our students are incorrectly recommended for LD services.

What do you see as major factors for your school's low scores on FCAT?

Georgine: Our score was partly lowered by the English component because of our large percentage of ESOL students who were just not proficient in English. Teachers were also not well prepared for teaching students to succeed on FCAT. We now have been improving the content and pedagogical knowledge of the teachers through the school's professional development program for the past few years. We are attending these workshops and improving our teaching.

Susana: Another factor is the poor parental involvement. I think the low-socioeconomic status of most of our parents, coupled with the lack of English language skills, makes it difficult for many to take advantage of the services that are available for preparing their children for schooling.

What recommendations would you make to a teacher who is about to begin teaching in your school?

Georgine: Our students need structure, so the teacher would need good classroom management skills and class rules that are acceptable to the students. Next, the teacher needs to be willing to accept and help students who are not academically ready to perform what is required of them. Our average student comes to us below grade level, so the teacher would need a strong belief in the NCTM statement emphasizing that all kids can learn in order to take our students from where they are to where they should be. Learning about the background of the students is also a must.

Susana: When I find myself getting frustrated by nasty four-letter words strewn around the room by students, I remind myself that in many of these students' backgrounds, these words occur often. If I were to send students to the office every time that occurred, they would miss a lot of work! My advice to a teacher would be to reprimand the student and/or schedule a meeting after class, but then, move on with the lesson. Keep the students learning in the classroom as much as possible.

COMMENTARY

Georgine's unit is rich in opportunities for helping students to enhance and extend their mathematical understanding of the important elements for displaying and interpreting data with bar graphs. Her requirement that students gather their own data, analyze the material, and then synthesize the results is highly recommended by NCTM's *Principles and Standards* (NCTM 2000), which advocates that students be engaged in problem-solving situations for which they have to "select and use appropriate statistical methods to analyze data." Middle school students should have problems where they need to "find, use, and interpret measures of center spread" (248).

Georgine's integration of assessment with instruction and the multiple opportunities she extends to students to perform well on the assessments help students internalize the key mathematical ingredients. Furthermore, her choice of investigating a health problem that plagues Latinos, Blacks, and Native Americans shows her attention to integrating cultural aspects into her lessons. More important is the information about diabetes that she is propagating among her students' families and friends.

As more leaders pull together to address issues of Latino and Hispanic populations, there is hope. For example, in April 2003, a national organization called TODOS: Mathematics for ALL became an affiliate of NCTM. Its goal is to provide leadership in the field of equity and mathematics education for all students with an emphasis on Latino/Hispanic students. Increasing equity awareness through scholarly and professional endeavors while identifying barriers to student achievement will guide its work. For further info, go to www.todos-mathematicsforall.org or write to TODOS, 9633 Callis Ct., Harrisburg, NC 28075.

Georgine also shows her respect for cultural differences in her students' approach to computation. Rather than require that students subtract "her way," she learns their way and, in turn, shares hers so that both she and the students enrich their mathematical base. An article by Perkins and Flor (2002) on algorithmic differences of immigrant students from Latin America recommends that teachers follow Georgine's approach, which is to "establish a sense of rapport in which both students and teachers are learners" (35). NCTM 2003 President Johnny Lott (2003) extends this rapport to students' families. He adds,

> Further, if we do not consider what and how a student learns outside of school and ignore family and community influences, we run a huge risk of making learning much more difficult for the student and mathematics irrelevant and impractical. . . . If we do not allow the child to do both, we are setting up a conflict between the students and us, between the student and family members and eventually between the family and us" (3).

Georgine's report that cooperative grouping works best with her ESOL students is also supported by research. Note that Georgine does include independent work and assessments because, she says, "students need to be able to work in both ways."

Research by Bustamante and Travis (1999) also supports her frequent use of manipulatives. In two predominantly Latino school districts, they report that both teachers and students found manipulatives useful for teaching mathematics; and, in their survey of teachers, 94% agreed that students benefit from the use of manipulatives. Findings by Lee and Jung (2004) show that students at different levels of bilingualism work best in groups because that strategy affords them opportunities to work in both languages. Even for those fluent in English, they conclude that small groups are beneficial for the development of metacognitive processes. From Georgine's overall classroom strategies and answers from discussion questions above, we can surmise that she adheres to the instructional guidelines recommended by Lee and Jung (2004) for assisting LEP students in learning mathematics. In addition to cooperative learning, these include: the use of multiple sources for representing the material such as graphic representations, manipulatives, and kinesthetic tools; the use of the students' native language to help them make sense of the mathematics; the development of language skills through questioning students and asking them to read and interpret graphs and other print materials; the creation of a supportive classroom environment; and accurate assessment of students' understanding.

Four months after my visit, Georgine e-mailed me to say that her school received not an "F" or a "D,", but a "high-C" rating on the FCAT! She wrote,

> I'm writing to tell you that we are officially off F list and are now a C school. The beautiful thing about it is that we are a high C—We didn't just barely make it! Our faculty and staff are overwhelmed with joy! None of my students passed, but they all showed progress. Hard work pays off, and now we are reaching for the stars. It's a wonderful feeling."

When I asked what she thought contributed the most to the good news, she responded,

> The reason we did so well this year is because we departmentalized, met often to plan, and attended a lot of professional development to enhance our content and pedagogical knowledge. We also had our students practicing FCAT strategies throughout the school year. It also helped a lot to require that our students formulate their own questions and work in groups."

The principal, Ms. McGinnis, was spotlighted in the local newspaper for the school's success. In the article, she attributes a large part of the success to community involvement. She says,

> The school had received the second 'F' at the close of the 2001–2002 school year. But that grade was not the final nail in our coffin. Instead, it sparked our rebirth. Our designation put us under the microscope of the state and media. The scrutiny had a galvanizing effect. The attention put us in the public spotlight and the public responded. Our school was inundated with offers for assistance and most were accepted. Individuals donated money that helped sponsor student activities . . . ; on any given day there were between 10 and 50 mentors and tutors at the school. Even our most disheartened faculty members could see that they were no longer in this fight alone. . . . Douglass Elementary is a testament to what can be achieved when schools and communities come together for children. . . . For me, "C" is an apt designation. It stands for the three most important factors in the school's success: cooperation, collaboration and community participation."

CONTACT

Georgine Roldan
Frederick Douglass Elementary School
314 NW 12 Ave.
Miami, FL 33169
Phone: 305-371-4687
E-mail: roldangermain24@yahoo.com

UNIT OVERVIEW:
FAVORITE MENU ITEMS AND HEALTH ISSUES

Aim: How can we protect ourselves from diabetes?

Objectives: Students gather data on foods to display on bar graphs and interpret.

Grade Levels: Fourth and fifth grades

Number of 50-Minute Periods: Three

Source: Original

Mathematics Principles and Standards Addressed:

♦ Principles for equity, curriculum, teaching, learning, assessment

♦ Mathematics as problem solving, communication, connection, reasoning, representation

♦ Data analysis, probability, and discrete math: Discover trends, formulate conjectures regarding cause-and-effect relationships, and demonstrate critical thinking in order to make informed decisions.

♦ Measurement: Apply appropriate techniques, tools, and formulas to determine measurements.

Prerequisites:

♦ Preliminary experiences with bar graphs

♦ Application of mean, median and mode

♦ Elements of types of food from the Food Pyramid

Materials and Tools: Per group: ruler, construction paper, and table of nutritional values from Taco Bell. Per student: homework sheet on diabetes given in Figure 5.2 and food content value in Figure 5.3.

Management Procedures:

♦ Assign students to groups of 3–5 to conduct activities and to solve problems.

♦ Have students develop and apply a rubric to assess the graphs.

♦ Assign students homework to replicate class activities for different data, and have them assess the results.

Assessment: Circulate to observe and question students' work. Check written work for accuracy in using formulas to find measures of central tendency. Have students use their rubric to assess the graphs. Review the diabetes questions of Figure 5.2 for accuracy.

6

TIM GRANGER: NATIVE AMERICANS AND INDIRECT MEASUREMENT

We are not the highest scoring school in the district, but we are not the lowest either. We have a lot of students who come to us not really ready for school. Their language skills are very low, and we have a high percentage of students who qualify for special education help. This is not uncommon with schools that have similar populations. We have a good number of students who come from poverty, from homes where there is abuse of some sort (chemical, physical, verbal, sexual), and from single-family homes. These things combine to provide some interesting challenges. The Aiming for the Stars unit of study has all of the components that I look for in a unit: high interest, solid mathematics, a possibility to integrate other curriculum areas, and the ability to pose a challenge to a large range of student abilities.

Tim Granger
Quil Ceda Elementary School, Marysville, WA

Tim Granger is a fifth grade teacher at Quil Ceda Elementary School, a suburban school of 600 students in grades K-5 located on the Tulalip Indian Reservation in northwestern Washington State. Tulalip is historically the original name of the tribe that lived on these lands. The tribe continues to exist to this day, although in smaller numbers. They were like most other Pacific Northwest tribes, getting their food from the Puget Sound and the abundant forests that lined its shore. The tribe used dugout canoes that were many feet in length (20 or more feet) for hunting and fishing. They continue to fish as a large part of their income, but they have also turned to casinos for additional income.

Quil Ceda Elementary School is a member of the Marysville School District in Marysville, Washington, located approximately 30 miles north of Seattle. Quil Ceda is a public school that serves a tribal population. The staff works hard to be certain that each student is successful. Tim's school population is derived

71

from the neighborhood with approximately 50% of his students qualifying for free or reduced-price lunches and with ethnicities of 25% Native American, 8% Russian, 4% Asian American, and the remainder Caucasian. All of the students from the tribe speak English. Their traditional language has nearly died out. Although there have been some limited attempts to bring this language back, it is not a widely spoken language. There are native teachers in the school, but none from the Tulalip tribes. There is a full-time Native American liaison, a member of the Tulalip tribe, who serves as an interface between the school community as a whole and the tribe.

Quil Ceda was built six years ago and is the newest school in the Marysville School District. The school is broken into four pods with either four or six classrooms in each pod. From the painting on the front peak of the school to the canoe hanging in the office (another of Tim's projects), the school is awash with art, the majority of which is Native American in design. Regardless of which culture it is, students are encouraged to embrace and share their culture with each other.

UNIT OVERVIEW

In this project, Tim's students construct and launch model rockets. He says, "Few events from my childhood stick out more than launching rockets with my family in the vacant lot near my home. The whoosh of the rocket as it lifted off towards the sky is something that will forever be a part of me. Little did I realize, however, how much mathematics was involved with those little model rockets." The models, manufactured by a company named Estes, are capable of over one thousand foot high flights. In the course of this project, the students learn to use the angle of their rockets' trajectory and even a bit of trigonometry to find the altitude their rockets reached. The students also use algebra to find out the velocity of their rockets. They convert the velocity into a number of different units, from feet per second to miles per hour. The rockets show the students the usefulness of algebra and trigonometry, something all too often forgotten in traditional programs—indeed, something also not easily found in most fifth grade programs.

How can Tim help his students apply trigonometric ideas when they have barely had algebra or have not even totally mastered the concepts of elementary number operations? Is he pushing his students to higher levels for which they are not prepared? And why? We can answer the last question quickly by asking another question: What are motivating activities for getting students to apply formulas in real life? So many of these activities, like determining how fast a toy car is accelerating down a ramp, require higher level math. In most texts, formulas are restricted to area, perimeter, or volume of geometric figures. If additional formulas are used, students are merely presented with the formulas and asked to find a missing variable. Tim takes on the challenge of making higher levels come to life for students so that they can apply them to challenging and motivating problems. Now, how does he do that with fifth graders? Read on!

Engaging Students

The unit starts with a bang when Tim takes his class out to the field and launches a rocket into the air. The students all crane their necks skyward in an attempt to see the rocket travel ever higher and then to follow as it falls gently back to earth on a parachute. As Tim repacks the rocket for another launch, he asks some questions: "How high did that rocket go? How fast did it go? Let's launch again and see if this flight is higher or faster than the first flight."

Another whoosh, another set of gasps, and his students are totally involved. The guesses of altitude and velocity flow freely from their mouths as they clamor to be the one who gets to chase after the rocket. Tim gathers the rocket and again asks more questions: "Did that flight go higher? Is there any way that we could figure out how high the rocket went on that flight? What about the speed? How fast did that rocket go? Oh, by the way, how does a rocket work? Let's launch once more and then go back into the classroom and answer some of these questions."

The final launch, the final recovery, the final set of questions. "How many of you would like to launch rockets?" The hands of the students shoot up like rockets themselves. They are hooked. They have accomplished the first goal of any successful math project; they are excited to be doing it.

Mathematics Lessons

When the students get back to the classroom, with the rocket as a prop, Tim goes over the questions again. How high did the rocket travel? Students respond with varying degrees of accuracy. The guesses for height range from 200 feet to 2000 feet; the guesses for speed range from 50 miles per hour to 1,000,000 miles per hour. These ranges play into the lesson perfectly. The class agrees that there needs to be a more accurate way of figuring out the altitude and velocity for each rocket than mere guessing. From here Tim turns to the overhead projector and draws a picture of a rocket launch, complete with a base line showing where the class stood and the path of the rocket. The resulting picture looks like an "L." Tim asks the class what shape they would get if he connected the top of the rocket flight (the top of the "L") with the class's location on the ground (the bottom of the "L"). Nearly everyone in the class replies that he would get a triangle.

Armed with this knowledge, Tim leads the students to the conclusion that if they knew how to find the height of the triangle, they could figure out how high the rocket traveled. The students quickly realize that it is not possible to measure the side of the triangle and that there must be another way of doing it. From previous conversations, Tim's students understand that if they know two out of three variables in an equation, then they can find the third. Next Tim discusses what parts of the triangle we *can* measure and identifies the triangle in question as a right triangle. The base distance comes pretty easily. Again, through guided discussion and use of a rocket-siting device (more on this later), the students find that they can measure the angle adjacent to the path the rocket took. Having established this discovery, Tim informs the students that there is a formula that they can use to find the altitude of a right triangle (see Figure 6.1). Tim points out,

> It is important to note that I ask the class to agree that all of our flights will be considered right triangles, and I ask them to agree to this verbally. The process of asking them to agree to something is very important as it shows the students that I value their opinions and their ideas. If a student disagrees, or cannot agree, the student feels welcome to express his/her ideas so that we can see how to address them.

FIGURE 6.1 ROCKET TRAJECTORY

Highest point rocket reaches

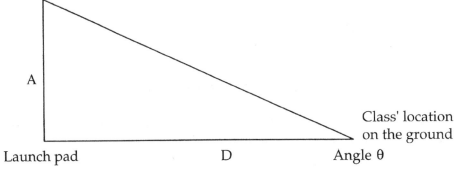

Launch pad   D   Angle θ

Tan θ = A/D
A = D Tan θ
A = Maximum altitude of the rocket
D = Distance from observer to launch pad
θ = Angle at highest altitude

After all the students have agreed, Tim introduces the formula which they call Mr. Granger's Formula: The height of the triangle is equal to the tangent of the angle multiplied by the base, or,

$$a = (\text{tangent of the angle})(\text{base}).$$

Initially, Tim asks them to believe that using the formula will give them the altitude of the right triangle. (Later, he will have the students use measurement to verify the relationships.) He draws a triangle on the overhead and has a student measure the length of the base (14 cm.). Next, another student uses a protractor and measures the angle as 36 degrees. Without explanation as to its origin, Tim passes around copies of his "Great Granny's Tangent Sheet" and directs the students to read the tangent of 36 degrees. Next, he plugs this value into the formula, uses a calculator, and declares that the altitude is 10.2 cm. Expecting and noticing some skeptics in the class, he invites a student to measure the altitude with a ruler. The subsequent measurement of 10.2 cm. convinces the class that Mr. Granger's formula "works."

Tim poses the question, "Do you suppose this formula works with lengths in inches as well as centimeters?" A couple of examples of formula use followed by measurement verification, using base lengths of various units, cements the ideas. Before the lesson closes, Tim asks the students when they would use this formula in daily life. Derrick offers, "To see how tall a building is." Ashley quickly follows with, "To see if a tree is big enough to fall on my house." Several students, recalling the opener for the unit, in chorus shout, "Rockets!" The room explodes with the same excitement as was generated by Tim's demonstration. As a wrap-up, Tim directs the students to stand and to join his chant. Clapping together and repeating the refrain, "the altitude is equal to the tangent of the angle times the base," the room rocks.

In order to provide the students with practice in finding the altitude of right triangles (and hence their rockets), Tim gives the students several lessons in which they actually use the formula to measure triangles. Tim takes the class out into the school's courtyard where he has drawn large triangles on the ground with chalk. Armed with protractors, calculators, and sheets of paper listing all of the tangents for angles from 1 to 90 degrees, his students in groups of two to three figure out the height of each triangle using their formula. Then they actually measure the height using a ruler. This physical confirmation shows them that the formula which they are using really does work. As the students work, Tim conducts group interviews, asking the students to explain the mathematical process used and how their answers were calculated. After they have measured triangles on the ground, he sends them to work on triangles that they cannot actually measure without the use of the formula. Tim asks them to find the height of trees that surround the school. The length of the base is given to them using a tape measure, and the angle is provided to the class using an electronic protractor mounted to a tripod. This tool will also be used as a rocket-siting device at the end of the unit. This process gives the students a great deal of practice with the formula in a way that they can relate to more than if Tim had simply given them numbers on a sheet of paper.

Tim's next challenge is to help students discover the velocity formula

$$(V = A/T),$$

with V being velocity, A being altitude, and T being the time in seconds. He lays out on the playground field several courses, each with a known but different distance. The students run the courses while he times them with a stopwatch. The students then determine which student is the fastest. By having different courses, the students are made to actually find the velocity of the students instead of just saying that the fastest student was the one with the shortest time. The students record it as Trial One, Trial Two, etc., and record distance and time. They then use this information to find their velocities.

After these races are completed, the class moves inside. Working in groups of three to four, the students find the velocity of toy cars. The cars are the pull-back type. The students pull them back, let them go, and time them over a known length of course. Tim's students also time a remote-controlled car as it travels down the hallway. The use of toys keeps the interest level high while giving the students practice in finding velocity. For further practice, the class again goes outside. With the help of another teacher standing on the school's roof about 20 feet above the ground, objects like stones, bananas, or shoes are dropped one at a time, and the travel time of each is recorded on the students' data sheets. The height above the pavement is measured and kept constant throughout. When the students return to the classroom, they compute the speed of each object using the distance-rate-time relationship.

Tim lets his students use calculators, and he turns on some classic rock 'n roll or delta-blues music as background inspiration. Comments like Rocio's, "I like dropping stuff off the roof. It's fun to see them bounce, and we can figure out how fast they fall!" or Breland's "The banana had a speed of 30 feet/second. Imagine!" convince Tim that his students are having fun and learning, too.

The next phase of the unit focuses on building the model rockets. Each student gets a model rocket kit to build his/her own rocket. Tim reviews the directions, highlighting any important parts. The students must have every phase of construction inspected to be certain that they have correctly completed that step (see Figure 6.2). The rockets generally take a week or so to build, paint, and dry. Finally, it is time to launch the rockets. Tim describes the launch:

> The rockets are launched on school grounds. A parent volunteer is located 150 feet from our launch site with the electronic protractor on the tripod. A second parent is located with the first as a timer and spotter. These parents also have a walkie-talkie. After a rocket is launched, the first parent sites along the top edge of the protractor (looking for the white puff of smoke that is sent out when the rocket ejects the recovery device) and then looks at the protractor. The parent reads the angle off

---

FIGURE 6.2 ROCKET QUALITY CONTROL CHECK-OFF

Directions: Check off when each item below is finished. Once your rocket is completely finished, have a teammate check off each quality control section as well. Fix any areas that are not checked off, and resubmit for final inspection.

You	*Partner*	*Teacher*	
			Fins are attached solidly.
			Fins are filleted.
			Nose cone comes off freely without sticking.
			Shock cord is firmly attached.
			Streamer is firmly attached.
			Launch lug is straight.
			Engine retainer ring is installed at the proper point (use the yellow tube to check).
			Engine retainer ring is installed securely.
			Rocket is decorated appropriately.

of the protractor and then radios this information back to the launch site, where a third parent writes the angle on a large form containing the students' names. The timer then radios back the time of flight to the launch site, which is also recorded. We generally run three different launchers in order to cut down on the time between flights.

After the launches are complete, the students come back into the classroom, and using the data collected from the field, they find the altitude and velocity of their rockets. Tim circulates around the groups as his students complete their calculations. "Did you see how fast mine went, Mr. Granger?" asks Mike. "How fast did it go, Mike?" "127.81 feet/second!" "Mr. G., mine went so high! It went 592.32 feet!" offers Jerry. The data from the class are taken and graphed using a computer spreadsheet program, and the results are compared. Next, the students write a final report telling all that they have learned about rockets, altitude, velocity, and mathematics (see Figure 6.3). Finally, the students complete a self-evaluation, describing what they did, how they did it, what they did well on, and what they would do differently the next time.

FIGURE 6.3 FINAL REPORT—SAMPLE OF STUDENTS' REPLIES

---

1. Describe how to find velocity.

    Ashley: The formula for velocity is V = A/T. The first thing you have to know to find velocity is the distance. If you were going to try to find the velocity of your friend running, you would time her running a distance. Then you would write down V = A/T. You could use a calculator and divide how far they ran and their time. Then that would be your answer.

    Shelby: You have to do a math formula. The formula is V = A/T. What the "V" stands for is velocity. The = means the V is equal to A/T. The "A" stands for the distance of something. The "/" means divided by, and the "T" means time. An example of the problem would be, say, the length was 55 feet, and the time was 2.05 seconds. You would divide those two numbers together and get the velocity. It would be 26.83 feet/second.

2. Describe how to find altitude.

    Jennifer: The formula for altitude is A = (tan angle) × B. That means you multiply the tangent by the base to get the answer. To find the tangent, you can find a button on a calculator to find the tangent you want. You do have to know what the angle is though.

    James: How you find the altitude is sort of like finding the velocity of something because you have to use formulas with both of them. The formula is A = (tan <) (B). What you do is get the tangent from the angle. Say the angle was 45 degrees; then the tangent would be 1.00. Then you would times that by the base. Say the base was 44 feet; the altitude is 44 feet.

3. How did you build your rocket?

    Kody: The first thing you need to do is read the directions and then find what you need and get it. Then you start with the first step, which is to check and see if your nose cone fits. Once you get to the fin attachment parts, you must fit them on right, or they will fall off. So the way I did it is by putting it on the table and let the table do the work while I put the fin on. When you get to the streamer part, you must do it right, or it won't fit in the cone.

4. What was the hardest part? Why?

    Joseph: The hardest part of my building my rocket was putting my wings on. I put glue on them, and they would only stay up for 5 minutes. Then they would just plop over. So I got very mad, but I tried a

---
FIGURE 6.3 FINAL REPORT (CONTINUED)

Joseph (Continued):

different no-run glue. It worked very well, so then my frustration was all gone.

Casey: There are a couple of things that were hard. One is putting the engine block in, 'cause if you don't put it in at the right measurement your engine will go through the rocket. And the other one is trying to do some of the measurements like the one for the engine block 'cause if you get it wrong, then the rocket won't work.

5.   What was the easiest part of the project? Why?

Shelby: The easiest part about building a rocket is probably putting it together. Even though it takes time, it can still be fun.

Joseph: The easiest part of doing this rocket has to be the test before the rocket launch—the altitude problems 'cause all you had to do is to get 90% correct or 9 out of 10. Then the other easy part was that I learned the altitude formula really well, so it was very easy.

6.   Is this project math, science, or both? Explain.

Derrick: I think this project has math and science. The science part has to do with launching the rocket just like if a real rocket were going into space. I also think this is math because you have to do a lot of calculations and have to do a lot of numbers. This whole rocket building process took time to figure out most of the calculations. It was hard work, but I like the math part of the rocket project.

Katie: I think this project was both math and science. This was like doing a science project because everyone did their fins differently. When we launch the rockets, we will be able to tell which way of putting the fins and the number of fins that works best. This is experimenting, which is science. The math part is using the altitude and velocity formulas to figure out how high and how fast the rocket went. That means that we had to use both math and science to figure out the best way to design and fly a rocket.

Kody: To me I think it is science because you are using formulas that are meant for science 'cause you need time and distance. I also think it is math, too. One reason is 'cause you need to measure all the different measurements like measuring the lines for the fins to go on and the measuring of the engine block to know where it needs to go. And, too, is 'cause you are using different instruments like a stopwatch and ruler to measure and time.

The rocketry unit closes with the viewing of the movie *October Sky*. This movie tells the story of a group of boys who grew up in a small coal-mining town and taught themselves about rocketry. Their knowledge leads them to winning a national science fair, earning college scholarships, and being able to leave their small town. Following the movie, Tim's students write letters to the main characters telling of their own rocketry experiences.

DISCUSSION BETWEEN COLLEAGUES

What is your philosophy of teaching mathematics?

My philosophy for teaching mathematics is simple. I believe deeply and truly that all children can be successful in mathematics if they are provided with the necessary motivation and scaffolding. I believe that children have a love of math, but many just do not know it yet. I believe that if I believe in my students and their ability, they will succeed. Finally, I believe that my role is to provide my students with lessons that are fun, engaging, and challenging while at the same time being their number one cheerleader.

Explain what you do in the lesson in the light of the cultural make-up of your students?

Because of my students' need for specific information regarding the usefulness of the information that they are learning, we spend a great deal of time working on the practical applications for the information. It is important for me to work to make the lessons not only applicable but also accessible. The lessons generally are scaffolded quite extensively in the beginning and then less so as the unit of study progresses. My units generally have a project component built in that provides a hands-on way of applying the knowledge they have gained.

What would you do differently if you taught this lesson to students of a different culture?

I would approach the unit somewhat differently. I have done the same unit for a mainly middle-class white group and spent more time on the abstract and on the algorithms and less time on the hands-on applications. With students from a higher socioeconomic level I would do more teaching of abstract concepts since I would not have to spend time with the background information that the students whom I have now, for example, are missing. As an example, on a recent field trip to Seattle, my students were amazed to see the Space Needle. Even though we live close by, my students had never seen it. Many of them are isolated from more mainstream experiences, so I have to probe what they have experienced before I can assume anything about their background.

Are there any teaching practices that you consistently apply based on the culture of your students?

> The concept of the "whole being greater than the one" is a part of the Native American culture at our school. I consistently use this worldview by having children work as part of a group toward a common goal. I also tend to tie the lessons into the world of my students. In the case of rockets, we not only find the altitude of the rockets, but also apply it to finding the height of trees. Lumber and the forests are a big part of our students' lives; therefore, they can see a real value in learning how to perform these measuring skills.

How did you come to understand your students' cultural background?

> Although I am not from the same culture as the Native American students in my class, I have a great appreciation for and a deep understanding of the culture. Growing up in Arizona, as well as spending a great deal of my time on the Hopi and Navajo reservations, has given me a greater understanding of the culture of my students. Although I am still an outsider, I have an appreciation for their culture that comes through to my students and their parents. I think the parents' acceptance of me shows up in the extent of their involvement with my class projects. They would not so eagerly come to school unless they trusted that I have their children's best interests at heart.

Tell us more about the parents' involvement in the project.

> My parents are an interesting mix of people. Most are from lower socioeconomic levels and many of them are not used to volunteering in the classroom. Parents come in 30 minutes or so before the launch (the launch traditionally takes place after lunch recess). During this time, they are trained on the use of the walkie-talkies and the protractor as well as a given quick overview of what is going to happen. I am very proud of the fact that a full one-third to one-half of my parents participate for any given project, including Native parents. In some cases, coming to my classroom is their first time in school for a positive experience.

How do you generally assess students?

> Students are assessed in a number of different ways, both formally and informally. The end result of their projects serves as an assessment (i.e., their rockets and finding the altitude and velocity of their

rockets). Observational information is also used in the assessment of my students. Finally, I spend a great deal of time talking with my students and asking questions of them while they are in the midst of their work. This is probably the most useful form of assessment that I use.

How does this lesson fit into your general curriculum?

> The Rocket Unit fills two very important needs in my classroom. First of all, it is a great way of getting kids to use formulas and to manipulate numbers. They see the way that formulas work along with the value of algebra. Second, it fills the need of being something very exciting for the kids to do that keeps them motivated at the end of the school year. It also serves as a culmination of all of the mathematics that we have done since the beginning of the year: multiplication, division, fractions, decimals, and geometry. Year after year, students of all levels, of all abilities and backgrounds, have been successful in this unit. One of the greatest things any teacher can hear is that his/her lessons made a difference. An e-mail I received from a former student just recently said it all. David said that because of the math that we did in fifth grade, he feels successful and smart in his math classes in middle school. What could be better?

What experiences using mathematical formulas have your students had prior to this unit?

> We work with a number of different formulas throughout the year. We use $s = h/m$ to find the strength-to-mass ratios of bridges we build; $a = (l)(w)$ to find the area of our gingerbread houses' walls and roofs; $x = c/d$ to find Pi; $p = (e/t)(100)$ to find the percent chance of an event occurring; and, of course, $v = d/t$ for velocity and $a = (\tan angle)(b)$ to find the altitude of a right triangle.

What recommendations would you make to a teacher who is about to begin teaching in your school?

> My first recommendation would be to value the culture of the students in your class. This is a key. Second, I would tell a new teacher not to fall into the trap of stereotyping students. These stereotypes, which include Native American students' being poor performers, can have a devastating effect of the performance of the students. Finally, I would urge a new teacher not to put artificial boundaries on the students. We often feel that fifth graders are not able to learn certain topics. I feel that all children can learn anything if they are provided with the necessary motivation and scaffolding.

COMMENTARY

The Center for Research on Education, Diversity and Excellence (CREDE) located at the University of California, Santa Cruz, is a "federally funded research and development program focused on improving the education of students whose ability to reach their potential is challenged by language or cultural barriers, race, geographic location, or poverty" (http://www.crede.ucsc.edu) Underlying CREDE's philosophy are two key tenets: "All children can learn" and "Children learn best when challenged by high standards." CREDE has established five standards for effective pedagogy:

- Teacher and students producing together

- Developing language across the curriculum

- Making meaning: Connecting school to students' lives

- Teaching complex thinking

- Teaching through conversation

It is clear that Tim adheres to the goals of both CREDE and NCTM in his teaching. CREDE's philosophy and standards are evident in his classroom. Mindful of his students' preferred learning style, which he describes as "tactile/kinesthetic with an emphasis on practical uses for the material they are learning," Tim designs a great number of hands-on projects, e.g., building a canoe, that tie into real life problems. Tim's assessment of his students' learning styles and his lesson designs are consistent with the recommendation of Bradley and Taylor (2002) to use hands-on experiences to build on American Indian and Eskimo children's learning preferences to develop their formal mathematics thinking. Desks in Tim's classroom are arranged to accommodate conversation between him and small groups of students on a regular and frequent basis. His frequent use of questioning, restating, praising, and encouraging assist the students' learning throughout the conversation.

CREDE's third standard concurs with an overarching goal of the NCTM *Standards* to integrate mathematics into familiar contexts, to mesh with students' personal styles, and to build on tasks of interest to the learner (NCTM 2000). Before his students embark on the job of building their rockets, Tim models for them as they watch the construction process. This observation-modeling process builds on the visual learning patterns common to American Indian learners (Tharp 1997). The assembly and launch of model rockets as the culmination of the unit not only provide motivation to learn mathematics but also connect to Tim's students' visual learning strengths and their need to produce demonstrable evidence of their learning. A wider context for learning mathematics is established as Tim helps his students apply their new mathematics understandings to the lumber and forestry industry, vital to the economics of their locale.

Instead of watering down the curriculum by emphasizing rote computation, Tim engages his students in tasks that incorporate algebra and trigonometry, concepts that may be deemed too advanced for fifth grade learners. As recommended in the equity principle of the NCTM *Standards*, Tim holds high expectations for his students, communicates these goals to his students, and supports his students with whatever assistance they need to meet their goals (NCTM 2000).

Tim integrates the curriculum by incorporating science concepts and language arts skills into the model rocket unit. According to Davison (2002), many educators maintain that "American Indian learners respond well to a thematically integrated curriculum" (23). Tim is convinced that this unit helps his students see their learning as a "whole," thereby finding meaning in the curriculum. Any accommodations Tim makes to ensure that his Native American students are successful make sense for all of his students. As Trumbull, Nelson-Barber, and Mitchell (2002) point out, "It is interesting that the approaches of indigenous peoples to teaching and learning coincide with some of the most highly touted elements of research-based instruction called for by our nation's education reformers" (8).

Tim puts a priority on student–student interaction because he maintains that "the students in my class tend to work better in small groups where there is a reliance upon each other for success." He and his students become a learning community as together they explore the concepts and master the skills required to successfully launch their model rockets. In their review of research studies detailing instruction of American Indian students, Hankes and Fast (2002) point out several principles that should guide mathematics instruction of Native American students. Key among these guiding recommendations is "cooperative rather than competitive instruction" (41). What is also evident to an observer of Tim's teaching is his enthusiasm, his love of mathematics, his creativity, and his sense of fun. He is a powerful catalyst for the motivation, enthusiasm, and success of his students, showing them the way to aim for the stars and walking with them on the journey.

CONTACT

Tim Granger
Quil Ceda Elementary School
2415 74th Street NE
Marysville, WA 98271
Phone: 360-653-0890
Fax: 360-651-0769
E-mail: Tim_Granger@msvl.k12.wa.us or tgranger10@aol.com
Website: http://www.msvl.k12.wa.us

http://www.mathforum.com/mathrich (the site I created
    regarding my math program, Creating Math Rich Students)

UNIT OVERVIEW:
AIMING FOR THE STARS: INDIRECT MEASUREMENTS AND ROCKETRY

Aim: How can algebra and trigonometry be used to help us find the speed and distance traveled by our model rockets?

Objectives: Students use trigonometry to find the altitude of right triangles. Given the distance and time traveled, students use algebra to find the speed.

Grade Levels: Fourth and fifth grades

Number of 90-Minute Periods: The unit takes place over three weeks and is usually taught three times a week for 90 minutes. Therefore, the total unit lasts nine lessons or so. This is somewhat variable depending on the class and the rate at which the students are learning the material.

Source: Teacher-developed, refined, and aligned with the NCTM and National Science Teachers Association (NSTA) standards.

Mathematics Principles and Standards Addressed:

♦ Principles for equity, curriculum, teaching, learning, assessment, technology

♦ Mathematics as problem solving, communication, connection, reasoning, representation

♦ Algebra: Represent and analyze mathematical situations and structures using algebraic symbols.

♦ Measurement: Apply appropriate techniques, tools, and formulas to determine measurements.

♦ Problem solving: Solve problems that arise in mathematics and in other contexts.

Prerequisites:

♦ Replacing variables with numbers in a formula

♦ Using a ruler, tape measure, protractor, and calculator

♦ Collecting and recording data

♦ A willingness to trust the teacher that the students will be guided through material that on the surface appears too difficult for them. This is really a key component to this lesson.

Mathematical Concepts: Students apply the distance–rate–time formula to find the speed of their model rockets. Students use the formula (altitude = tangent of the angle × base) to find the altitude reached by their model rockets.

Materials and Tools: Per group: ruler, tape measure, protractor, calculator, table of tangent values, stopwatch, assembled model rocket. Per class: rocket launch system, electronic protractor, walkie-talkie, videotape of *October Sky*.

Management Procedures:

- Assign students to groups of 2–4 to conduct activities, to assemble model rockets, and to solve problems.

- Engage parent/teacher volunteers to assist with building and launching rockets and with other activities as needed.

- Assign exercises for practice in applying formulas to find speed and altitude.

- Give very clear guidelines regarding behavior and performance to the students.

Assessment: Circulate to observe and question students' work. Check written work for accuracy in using formulas to find speed and altitude. Use checklist to assess rocket quality control. Use a paper-and-pencil test covering the mathematics content of the unit. Have the students write about the project that they do. This writing can take the form of a letter to their parents explaining the project. Administer a self-assessment at the end of all of the projects. This self-assessment asks the following questions:

What was the easiest part of the unit for you? Why?

What was the hardest part of the unit for you? Why?

What would you do differently next time? Why?

What grade do you think you deserve? What reasons can you give to justify your answer?

7

RENOTE JEAN-FRANÇOIS: HAITIANS AND TECHNOLOGY

The concept of equity-digital divide has taken on new meaning. It is no longer limited to the student-to-computer ratio. Equity also encompasses the way this technology is being used with at-risk students versus advanced ones. My concern that many at-risk students are having little experience with technology led me to devise ways to help my Haitian students address various needs such as the need to be proficient in digital-age tools and ways, the ability to think creatively and logically, and the ability to assess and redirect one's thinking.

Renote Jean-François
Wilson Middle School, Dorchester, MA

Although most Haitian-Americans live in the larger cities such as Boston, New York, and Miami, they also live in cities and towns throughout the United States. In the Boston Primary Metropolitan Statistical Area, the 2000 U.S. Census data counts 43,819 Haitians (www.census.gov). How are schools addressing the needs of these students? Josiane Hudicourt-Barnes, a Haitian researcher at TERC, highly recommended Renote Jean-François as a bilingual teacher of Haitian students who demonstrates exemplary answers to that question. In Boston, TERC has researchers at the Chèche Konnen Center, which is Creole for "search for knowledge," studying the ways that children's cultures can influence their learning of mathematics and science (www.projects.terc.edu.cheche_konnen).

Renote teaches at an urban school situated on a hill in a low-income section of Boston called Dorchester. Wilson Middle School draws students from other low-income areas such as Hyde Park, Mattapan, and Roxbury. As a Title 1 school, its population is largely African American with the remaining students coming from the Caribbean area. Renote teaches the 15% of entering middle grade Haitians who are classified as ESL literacy students. They are placed in a self-contained class and are taught the subjects in their native language except for English, for which they use 70% native language and 30% English at the beginning of the year. The percentages are reversed near the end of the year.

Renote explains, "This is not to be confused with bilingual instruction in which students receive ESL instruction and content area instruction in English and their native language." Renote's students have had no or limited schooling prior to their arrival in the U.S. They are not proficient in English, and they attend the literacy class until they are ready to enter regular bilingual classes, usually in two, sometimes three years. While some students have been in her class for almost two years, others have been there for less than one. She adds,

> A typical student in my class enters having had disrupted schooling due to the political unrest as well as other counterproductive situations typical of impoverished countries. As a result, they may be of middle school age, but, academically, they are functioning at a first- to third-grade level. As one might expect, they lack self-confidence and show resistance to approaches allowing them control and/or autonomy. They tend to depend on me to tell them what to do in most circumstances, and, in an attempt to hide academic gaps, they often refuse to try anything on their own. This attitude also is evident in their thinking process. When faced with a problem deemed somewhat difficult, they have one of two responses: "I can't do it, because I don't understand" or "Let me ask somebody to do it for me." Now, this is not true of all of our entering Haitian students. Some enter on grade level and really excel in math. Indeed, those students typically outperform our American students on the state's Stanford test.

The real challenge for Renote is to get her students on grade level in three years so that they can be mainstreamed into bilingual classes. For her 15 students, she provides instruction mostly in Haitian Creole, except for the ESL period where English is the focus.

UNIT OVERVIEW

Renote has three major goals for the unit described in this profile. She wants to help her students to develop a conceptual understanding of angles and their measures, apply their knowledge of angles to programming a robot to follow the course of the Haitian revolution on a map, and employ critical thinking skills by developing their own higher level questions and redirecting their thinking when necessary.

PREPARATORY ACTIVITIES

Renote begins the lesson by reviewing homework requiring students to determine angles, polygons, and lines that can be formed with their body parts. The entire lesson, with a few exceptions of students interjecting an English word or two, is in Creole. Renote begins by asking students to share examples of their angles and polygons.

Jean: When I spread out my legs like this, I form an angle.

Marie: Look at the angles I can form with my arm and elbow. *(She makes her arm parallel to the floor and moves her elbow back and forth.)* I can make my elbow perpendicular to my arm.

Yves: I can form a triangle with my two legs and the floor.

Iraniece: When I lie down on my bed, I can form a triangle with my torso, legs, and arms.

Renote: Take out your manipulatives with the different-sized polygons. Now, let's go back to Marie's use of her elbow and arm to form different-sized angles. Marie, can you model a right angle for us?

Marie makes a right angle with her arm, and Renote says, "Find a right triangle among the polygons, and place your finger on its right angle." She walks around to check students' angles and asks, "What do we call angles that are greater than 90 degrees?" No one responds, so Renote tells students the names and then has them use a right triangle from their set of polygons as a model to determine acute and obtuse angles from among the angles of the polygons on their desks.

She introduces the protractor and has students practice using it for determining the degrees of angles. She distributes a handout for students to measure angles with protractors, and she walks around to see if students understand the key ideas. She has students discover that the sum of the consecutive angles of a parallelogram is 180 degrees and then introduces the terms *supplement* and *supplementary angles.* Her assessment tells her that students do have a good grasp of the types of angles and their measures, so she tells the students that they are now ready to begin programming a robot called Roamer to move around the room. Looking like a big M&M candy, Roamer is a battery-powered robot that can be programmed to follow Logo commands. (For a picture and description of the Roamer, see www.Terrapin Logo.)

On the following day, she gives the students a pretest that will also serve as a posttest six weeks later (see Figure 7.1). During the social studies period she assigns students readings on Haitian history and has them (1) identify 4–8 key persons and their roles in the Haitian Revolution; (2) identify the date and place of the creation of the flag and the person who sewed it; (3) take notes, paying attention to what, who, when, where, and why; and (4) discuss the notes in small groups and with the whole group. Her plan is to have students work on programming at least three times a week during the data collection period, which will last six weeks. Depending on the topic being studied, students will design pathways with various stops of different duration. They will next program the robot to go along the path. To meet their objectives, students must anticipate possible problems and make consequent

FIGURE 7.1 PRETEST/POSTTEST IN ENGLISH AND HAITIAN CREOLE

Read the following prompts carefully; then ask and write at least three questions that will help you understand each situation better. Write your comments about each situation.

Li sitiyasyon yo ak atansyon, poze epi ekri pou pi piti twa kesyon k ap ede ou konprann li pi byen. Ekri kòmantè ou sou chak sitiyasyon.

1. Edward saved money for months to buy a bike. He took his time to assemble it and went out to try it for the first time. As he was riding it down the hill toward his house, he realized that the bike was starting to go faster and faster. He tried to slow down, but the brakes didn't seem to work. Edward had to think fast. Straight ahead there were some broken pieces of glass; on one side of the path he saw his 5-year-old cousin playing; on the street side, a car was backing up.

    Edwa pase plizyè mwa ap sere lajan pou I achte yon bisiklèt. Li pran san I pou li ranje bisiklèt la epi I al eseye monte yon premye fwa. Pandan I ap desann mòn ki mennen lakay li a, li wè bisiklèt la kòmanse ale vit vit. Li eseye ralanti men fren yo pa mache. Edwa bezwen reflechi rapidman. Tou dwat devan I gen yon pakèt moso boutèy, sou yon bò li wè ti kouzen I ki gen 5 an k ap jwe, sou bò lari a gen yon machin k ap fè bak.

2. Marc thought of an idea to experiment with how motion works. He took a rubber band, rolled pieces of paper into small balls, and started throwing them at other students. The teacher made him stay after class to clean up the room. Marc got upset and said, "It's not fair."

    Mak gen lide fè yon eksperyans pou wè ki jan mouvman mache. Li pran yon elastik, li fè ti boulèt papye epi li kòmanse kalonnen yo sou lòt elèv. Pwofesè a fè I rete apre lekòl pou netwaye klas la. Mak fache li di «se pa jis sa».

3. Imagine that you are the teenaged son/daughter of a French colonist living in St. Domingue around 1802 in the midst of the slave revolt. Write three questions that you would ask your parents and a runaway slave to help you understand what is going on.

    Imajinen ou se pitit fi/gason yon kolon fransè k ap viv nan Sendomeng vè ane 1802 yo, nan moman revòt esklav yo. Ekri twa kesyon ou ta mande yon nèg mawon pou ede ou konprann sa k ap pase a.

FIGURE 7.1 PRETEST/POSTTEST IN ENGLISH AND
HAITIAN CREOLE (CONTINUED)

4. If you were the teenaged son/daughter of a slave or freed slave, what questions would you have asked?

    E si ou te piti fi/gason yon esklav oubyen yon afranchi, ki kesyon ou ta mande?

5. Josh is going Christmas shopping. His mother gave him three twenty dollar bills. He wants to have enough money left over to buy flowers for his girlfriend's birthday.

    Josh pral achte kado nwèl. Manman I ba li twa billè ven dola ak kat biyè dis. Li vle gen lajan rete pou li achte flè pou fèt menaj li.

6. Here are the results of one of the experiments we did in class. What questions come to your mind when you look at the data in the graph? (Ask at least three questions.)

    Men rezilta yon esperyans nou te fè nan klas la. Lè ou gade enfòmasyon nan tablo grafik sa a, ki kesyon ki vin nan tèt ou? (twa kesyon pou pi piti.)

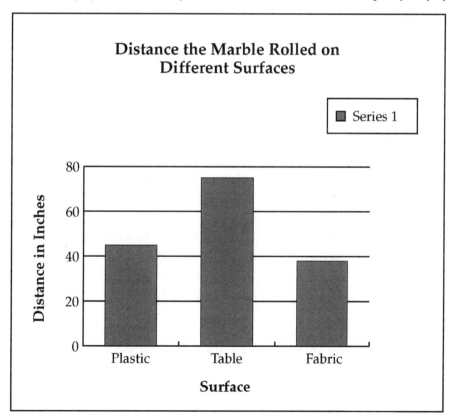

plans. If the outcome is different from the expected one, they will have to reevaluate their plan to determine why and then to make the necessary modifications. They will then reflect on the process in their journals and verbally submit a group report on their achievement.

The next day finds students eagerly entering class to see what this robot unit will entail. Space for the teams to experiment with the Roamer is not large because the classroom is quite small. Putting some desks out in the hall and letting students use the chairs helps. Yves says, "My brother said there is a computer inside the Roamer. Is it true?" Renote replies, "Maybe you will be able to determine that for yourself, Yves."

For the next lessons, Renote uses the math and social studies periods for this project because her intention is to have students direct Roamer to trace a path taken by Haitian patriots during the Haitian revolution of 1791. She first focuses on helping students understand the Logo language, as well as developing the understanding that Roamer responds to specific instructions. Holding the Roamer up high, Renote leads the class in a discovery of its properties:

Renote   What do you suppose this is?

Jeanne: A toy.

Claude: A machine.

Renote   Can you describe it?

Yves: It's round. It has numbers and arrows on it.

Jean: It also has letters, on and off buttons, and wheels.

Having done that, Renote says, "Let's practice giving commands to each other and executing them before we work with the Roamer. Tell me how to go around this table. I will keep my eyes closed, and I will do exactly what you tell me." Students give commands that at first have Renote bumping into tables or going too far from the targeted table. They then analyze what happened during the process and tell Renote that her "steps were too long" or the she "turned too quickly." Renote then tells students that it is her turn to give directions and that they are to pay particular attention to any differences they observe between her directions and those that she was told to follow. As Renote calls out directions to a student volunteer, the students notice that Renote's directions are very specific: she indicates how big each step is, how many steps to take in each direction, and when a 90-degree turn should be made. She then has the students try to give her directions again to go around the table. Once successful, she discusses the meaning of each symbol on the Roamer, and, in small groups, they write simple programs on the computer and then download them to the robot. They first have Roamer trace squares and rectangles through simple programs like FD 1, RT 90, FD 1, RT 90, FD 1, RT 90, FD 1. Students then spend thirty to forty-five minutes a day planning, conducting, and analyzing activities with the Roamer. Everyday, they write reflections on the activities in their journals.

ENGAGING STUDENTS

Renote explains the assignment to the students by telling them that Roamer has to pass through various towns on the map of Haiti to retrace the steps of a messenger during the Haitian Revolution. The order of the towns is Cap Haitien, Gonaives, Petite Rivière de l'Artibonite, Saint Marc and Arcahaie. She shows the class a large map of Haiti that measures 4' × 6' and has the towns listed (see Figure 7.2). Placing this map on the floor, she then assigns students to groups. Each group of four to five students will have a Roamer and will need someone assigned to (1) lead and take notes of the programming ideas; (2) type the program; (3) monitor the Roamer closely to see how closely it adheres to the program; and (4) lead the discussion on revisions, and, if necessary, take notes. Renote purposely does not give specific examples or directions on how to carry out these steps because she wants to allow the students opportunities to brainstorm and develop their own plans.

FIGURE 7.2 MAP OF HAITI

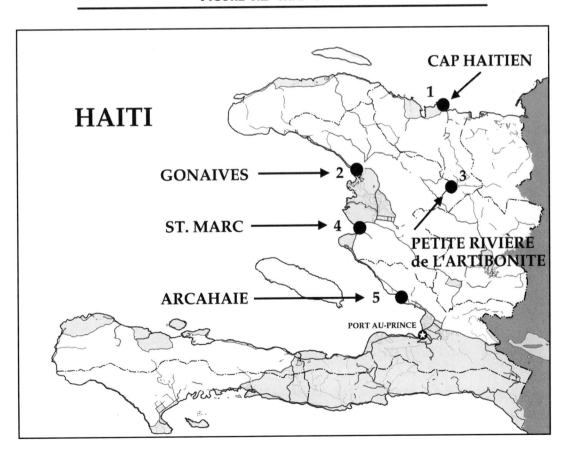

Although each team approaches the assignment differently, they all fail on the first attempt. One team starts to program right away and finds that Roamer does not go as planned. A second team prefers to wait for the enlarged map to measure the distances between the stops before they start, but their measurements are off. The third team works with a small map and makes visual predictions that are way off target. Throughout the unit, Renote observes student inter-action during activities and records comments and questions they explore with their team members to determine later whether they were asking higher-level questions. As the students work in groups, she hears the following comments:

Group 1

Iraniece: OK. Roamer has to start at Cap Haitian and end up at Arca-haie. She could go forward straight there, then make a turn to get to Petite Rivière de l'Artibonite. (*She uses the map on the bulletin board to show the path.*)

Jacques: It looks like it has to make an almost 45-degree left turn to get to here.

Claude: How many steps do you think it might take to get there?

Jacques: I don't know. Let's guess five and just start programming.

Iraniece: (*She types*): FD 5, RT 90, FD 1, RT 50, FD 3, RT 40.

Mikaelle: That is not working. It is going too far out, and it is turning the wrong way. We must make the steps smaller and check the angles.

Jacques: Well, it goes forward, then makes a left turn, and goes for-ward again.

Iraniece: Yeah. Let's see what happens. (*Fails.*)

Claude: Well, the program didn't work. I think we planned it correctly, but the Roamer did not do the turns the way it was supposed to. How come?

Group 2

Marie: Let's just put it on the direction of Gonaives and move it, say, two steps, then have it turn 90 degrees to get to the Petite Rivière de l'Artibonite.

Patrick: OK. Then it has to move a shorter distance and make a smaller turn, like one step and maybe 45 degrees.

Jeanne: And then the rest is straight down. So let's just try this: FD 2, LT 90, FD 1, RT 45, FD 1, LT 90, FD 2. (*She types, and the group ob-serves the Roamer not doing the expected.*)

Yves: Why is it doing that? Look at how little it turns for the 45 de-grees. Let's try different angles.

Group 3

Serge: Let's just start to program and see what happens?

Carlos: OK. Suppose we try FD 1, LT 90, FD 1, RT 60, FD 1, LT 35, FD 2.

Nicette: That did not work. We need to look at the map more closely.

After each session, Renote tells the students to write reflections on their attempts and outcomes, and she notices very little writing being done. But, from their experiments, students know what they need to know and what tools would be useful to them:

Marie: Ms. Renote, we need to know how to change the unit of distance of the Roamer because it is going too far. We want to make it go a shorter distance at a time.

Renote shows students how to change the default unit to a distance of 20 cm. Students modify and try their programs again, but the angles are the next problem.

Yves: How can we make Roamer trace angles other than 90 degrees?

Renote: Did you try to use its compass? *(The compass is a piece of 8" × 11" paper with various angles and a little turtle pinned in the center. As you turn the turtle, it indicates the angle that it traces.)*

Claude: Yes. We tried it, but it didn't work. Here is what we did. We placed Roamer on Cap Haitien facing the first town. Then we used this program, but the angles are messed up. *(He shows it on the board.)*

FD 2, LT 50, FD 3, RT 50, FD 3, LT 90, FD 3.

Renote: Let's look at the Roamer go through Claude's group programming again, and then we will try to trace the path on the board.

As students observe the path, Renote tells Nicette to trace the actual path of the Roamer and Claude to trace the desired path (FD 2, LT 50, FD 3) on the board from Gonaives to Petite Rivière de l'Artibonite. (See Figures 7.3 and 7.4.)

FIGURE 7.3 ACTUAL PATH OF ROAMER FROM GONAIVES

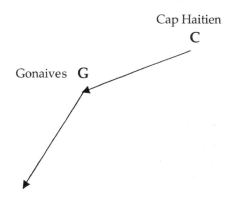

FIGURE 7.4 DESIRED PATH OF ROAMER FROM GONAIVES

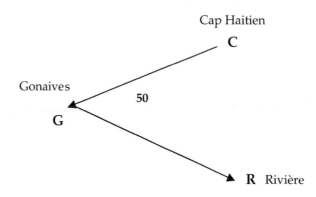

Renote says, "Let's see if we can determine what is going on here. Any ideas?" The students are silent, so she says, "Let me give you two hints. The first is a question: Which direction is Roamer facing when it has reached Gonaives?" The students point to the arrow tip at point G. Renote continues, "Here is the second hint: If Roamer were to continue going in that direction, what would its path look like on the board? Use dotted lines to show this imaginary path from the desired path figure " "I can show you," Iraniece says, as she draws Figure 7.5.

FIGURE 7.5 DOTTED PATH OF ROAMER CONTINUING STRAIGHT AHEAD FROM GONAIVES

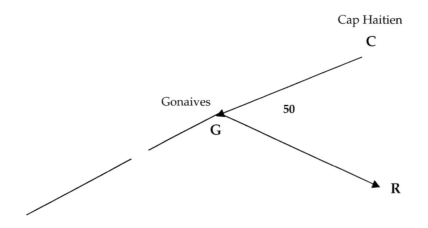

Renote: Good. Thank you. Now look carefully at Figure 7.5 to figure out what Roamer will do if you tell it to turn left 50 degrees. Marie, please come and be Roamer facing this direction on the floor map. Will your turn look like Figure 7.3 or Figure 7.4?

Marie: I know it will be like Figure 7.3, Ms. Renote, because the turn in Figure 7.5 is much greater than 50 degrees."

Renote says nothing while she lets the students think about what all this means. Then she asks, "How wide a turn would Roamer have to make to land on the ray GR?

Jeanne: The straight line is 180 degrees, so subtract that from 50 degrees to get 130 degrees.

Renote: That is the idea, but remember that a straight line is not an angle. What do we call an angle whose rays are on a straight line?

Jeanne: Oh, that is a straight angle.

Renote then reminds the students that angles whose sum is 180 degrees are called supplementary angles.

Renote: Let Roamer be positioned at Gonaives and suppose we want it to make a 40-degree turn instead of that 50 degrees. What turn should it do?

Yves (lost in thought and unmindful of Renote's question):   That means, if we want it to go 75 degrees, then we have to tell it to go 105 degrees. Isn't that right Ms. Renote?

Renote: Test it out, and if you are right, please share your discovery with the others.

Having received answers to their questions, the students are energized to try again and practice their new skills. They reprogram the Roamer and succeed almost immediately. Renote invites Claude to write his successful program on the board:

FD 2, LT 140, FD 3, RT 130, FD 2, LT 90, FD 2.

ASSESSMENT

Renote's assessment consists of the pre- and post-paper and pencil test, together with student observations and comments that she noted throughout the unit. She also noted the number of times students asked higher-level questions. Although changes in self-confidence were not readily evident while dealing with other content areas, Renote noticed that the students progressively demonstrated more confidence when programming the Roamer. Even the shy students tended to take a more active role or even emerged as leaders during the activities. She noted these as signs of a certain intellectual independence. Her notes show evidence of students' demonstrating higher levels of thinking and also geometric understanding. Expansion on these aspects is in the discussion.

DISCUSSION BETWEEN COLLEAGUES

What is your philosophy of teaching mathematics?

> Mathematics should be taught in a way that allows students to see its usefulness in their lives while helping students acquire other necessary skills.

Do you lecture at times?

> Boston public schools, in general, are moving away from this practice. We use block scheduling in my school. That would make a traditional class quite boring for students. We use the workshop model in which a class is subdivided into sections and activities lasting no more than 20 minutes. This year my math class is structured as follows: (1) an open response question, which they first try to answer alone, followed by their sharing ideas with a partner and then with the whole class; (2) homework review; (3) a mini lesson; (4) practice; (5) homework assignment; and (6) reflection on what they've learned.

How does your school place literacy students?

> If students fail the entrance exam, they take the literacy test to determine whether they are low performing or literacy students. Haitian students are tested for reading and basic math in Creole. There also is a test in French for students who are not fluent in reading and/or writing Creole. If such students cannot function in the regular bilingual program, well, that is when they come to me.

What are the preferred learning styles of your students? How do you accommodate for these styles?

> These students come from a system in which memorization is the focus. While they are with us, they progressively discover their learning styles. When they first arrive, they are usually very, very dependent. To accommodate them, we use discussions, different reading strategies, graphic organizers, and hands-on activities.

Explain what you do in the lesson in the light of the cultural make-up of your students?

> As much as possible, I try to find ways to build their self-esteem. My students not only are way behind their grade level but also are bombarded by negative images from the media about Haitians. I stress that we are a proud people and that we have made and continue to make great contributions to society. They are all surprised, for example, to

learn from your article (Germain-McCarthy, 2001b) that Haitians have affected many facets of New Orleans' culture or that the African American museum in Chicago is named after the Haitian, Jean Baptiste Du Sable, who founded Chicago.

Are there any teaching practices that you consistently apply based on the culture of your students?

I do a lot of small and large group discussions because our culture is more oral. They consistently have to write down the results of their discussions in order to learn to function in their new environment. I have them do problems through think-pair-share cooperative activities that require them to first think about it, then share with someone else, and then extend that to the whole group. Collaborative grouping also works well because back home the "coumbite" is the pillar of the rural communities and means everyone sticks together. Thus, every member helps the community move forward by helping those in need.

What would you say is most challenging for your students?

The students bring to school rich personal experiences. However, they are overwhelmed by the vast amount of information they have to process in their effort to deal with the cultural shock and by learning the rules required to function in a new academic setting. In their previous schooling experiences, they did not have a voice because of the linguistic barrier; they knew very little French but were expected to converse in and to read French in their schools. They also come from a teacher-centered, rote-learning environment in Haiti to the more open-ended and critical-thinking environment that I like to foster. Initially, they come lacking self-confidence together with an accompanying reliance on the teacher to tell them what to do, to ask questions for them, and even to articulate their thoughts. Therefore, thinking critically, solving problems, and managing a minimum of intellectual independence are very challenging for them. However, they can be helped to develop these skills.

In general, what did you learn from the assessments and your observations?

The results of the pretest and of the posttest showed no significant difference, again because writing is not their strong area. Aside from the comments in the posttest, "yes/no" questions appear in greater numbers in the students' responses to the situations presented in both the pretest and posttest.

Questions and comments I recorded during observations of small group discussions seem to show in-depth thinking. Students also persevered because they were interested in finding answers. On analysis, their journal entries did not reflect the in-depth discussions that took place in the planning and analysis processes. Most students had very few comments on the discussions. However, it is not surprising since these are literacy students who are still struggling with their writing.

What are your views on ESL students and technology usage?

In school systems that have begun to address some of the technology issues, decision makers are not clear on how to best use technology to benefit at-risk students. Students fall under the category of at-risk because of one or a combination of the following: socioeconomic status, gender, race, limited English proficiency, special needs, or low academic performance. Of these, students in bilingual and ESL programs appear to be at the bottom of the ladder. ESL and bilingual students quite often fall into several, rather than just one, of these categories. They are swept aside unless they are able to make their voices heard with high test scores or performances in math, science, or technology. On their own initiative, teachers in bilingual programs often have to adjust to what has been decided for the mainstreamed students. There are not enough studies done on the effects of integrating technology into the broader curriculum; there are even fewer studies on technology and the development of specific skills like critical thinking. Among those studies completed, surveys and case studies are over-represented. Their focus is mainly on identifying factors that explain the presence of technology.

What recommendations would you make to a teacher who is about to begin teaching in your school?

I would recommend that he or she read about Haitian history to understand that a student coming from a country of unrest may perform at two to three years below grade level and yet be very bright. I have some very smart kids in this class. The history also needs to be shared with the students so that they come to learn that their ancestors' contributions are still appreciated today.

COMMENTARY

Advice found in the literature reviewed in chapter 3 of this book for teaching students from low-performing or diverse backgrounds is to be aware that such students may be at a disadvantage in a reformed-based classroom. Research indicates that, historically, schools have had low expectations for these students, so teachers have underestimated their capacity to engage in challenging activities requiring higher order thinking. Furthermore, the students' exposure to technology, if any, is limited to drill and practice, learning to use tool software, and playing games (Means, 1991). Courses such as web design or programming are often not accessible to at-risk students. Such exclusion increases the likelihood that they will be at risk of not becoming literate. But what does literacy mean in the 21st century? According to the North Central Regional Educational Laboratory (www.NCREL), it is no longer just basic literacy, but "digital literacy." This literacy includes and extends beyond traditional basic literacy to include scientific literacy (ability to understand and apply personal decision making to civic and cultural affairs and economic productivity); technological literacy (competency in the use and application of computers and networks); visual literacy (ability to use and interpret 21st century media resources to enhance the problem solving process); economic literacy (ability to determine elements that affect the course of an economic problem, their expected consequences, and the gathering and interpretation of data to weigh costs against benefits); information literacy (ability to locate, coordinate, and apply a range of media using technology, communication networks, and electronic resources); multicultural literacy (ability to know and appreciate one's culture as well as those of others); global awareness (recognition and understanding of interrelationships among international organizations, sociocultural groups, and individuals across the globe). The lack of access to and proficiency in these skills creates a gap which is described by NCREL as follows:

> In the 1990s, the digital divide was characterized as a gap in technology access that translated into inequities in educational, economic, social, and civic opportunities among sectors of the population. Since then, education leaders have come to realize that access is simply the first step. Equally important are robust home access and the readiness of individuals to use technology, communication networks, and information efficiently, effectively, and productively (http://www.ncrel.org/engauge/skills/divide.htm).

Reports on robotics programs indicate positive outcomes because they allow the integration of practically all the other subjects and offer students the opportunity to develop various skills, including thinking skills and team skills, which are essential for the workforce in the 21st century. Renote's unit demonstrates the integration of oral and written language, history, math, and visual and creative arts, while students practice the socialization skills necessary to solve problems in teams.

Renote's concern that her students will lack technological skills motivates her to create and assess a unit requiring precisely what her students are not prepared to do based on their cultural learning experiences—critical thinking that is creative, logical, and able to redirect itself. She creates high expectations for her students by having them engage in the process of programming that requires analytical thought and is typically reserved for high-achieving students. Furthermore, the precision and mental discipline required for programming constitute lifelong assets that are useful in the academic setting as well as in everyday experience, and she wants her students to develop these skills.

By keeping careful records of her students' approaches to problem solving in various situations and by having them do pre- and posttests, Renote collects and analyzes the data to conclude that her students are capable of engaging in higher level thinking. Indeed, she concludes, "The assessment of the unit shows that, contrary to the trend, courses like programming are accessible to at-risk students and that these students are able to engage in tasks requiring higher level thinking."

It is noteworthy to discuss Renote's direct teaching of the geometry content with manipulatives. Through research investigating geometric thinking, Fuys, Geddes, and Tischler (1988) showed that a model for the learning of geometry developed by Dutch mathematics teachers Pierre and Dina van Hiele largely describes the way students learn geometry. The model identifies five levels of thinking in geometry. At level 0, the recognition stage, students can recognize, construct, draw, or copy shapes as a whole. At level 1, the analysis stage, they are able to analyze shapes, formulate their definitions, and discover their properties. At level 2, the ordering stage, students are able to use the definitions and properties of figures to formulate informal proofs about these figures and their properties. At level 3, the deduction stage, students formally prove theorems deductively; and at level 4, the rigor stage, they can rigorously compare different axiomatic systems.

The model asserts that students must progress through a lower level before attaining the next higher one, and that progression through the levels is determined not by chronological age, but by appropriate instructional experiences. The study supports the idea that each level has its characteristic language and that instruction at an inappropriately high level may explain some of the difficulties that secondary school students experience with geometry. Results of the study also demonstrate that the use of concrete materials and manipulatives can motivate students to play with their ideas and to become more reflective as they process varying ways of thinking. Beginning with the students' own bodies, Renote provides students with the van Hieles' informal experiences at levels 0 and 1, experiences that they need but may not have had. By guiding students through the investigations with the manipulatives, she helps them to develop or reinforce their understanding of important definitions and relationships at level 2. She leads students deeper into level 2 reasoning by having them apply their knowledge to measure with a protractor and to program Roamer.

Hollebrands' (2004) research indicates that while high school students are comfortable performing rotations of 0, 90, 180, and 270 degrees, they make errors when determining how to turn a figure about a center of rotation for different degrees—errors much like those Renote's students made trying to turn the Roamer a given degree. Renote's approach holds promise for her students to gain access to the type of thinking required for geometry at level 3, so they will be better prepared for high school.

In an interview conducted by Rogers Hall (2001), teacher–researcher Josiane Hudicourt Barnes at TERC's Chèche Konnen Center comments that linguistically and culturally diverse students show a "great capacity for understanding difficult mathematics and science content when their teachers create learning environments that give them space to explore and express their ideas" (5). Renote's unit is an example of Hudicourt Barnes' words in action.

CONTACT

Renote Jean-François
Wilson Middle School
18 Croftland Avenue
Dorchester, MA 02124
School phone: 617-635-8827
Fax: 617-635-6414
E-mail: renotejf@msn.com

UNIT OVERVIEW: THE ROAMER AND THE HAITIAN REVOLUTION

Aim: How can we apply geometric concepts to programming a robot?

Objectives: Students will approximate the measures of angles and distances and use that information to integrate Haitian history and technology to the task of programming.

Grade Levels: Fifth and sixth grades

Number of 60-Minute Periods: Eight to ten

Source: Original

Mathematics Principles and Standards Addressed:

- Principles for equity, curriculum, teaching, learning, technology

- Mathematics as problem solving, communication, connection, representation

- Geometry: Understand patterns, relations, and functions.

- Measurement: Apply appropriate techniques, tools, and formulas to determine measurements.

Prerequisites:

- Previous experience using the computer: students should know how to operate the computer.

- Knowledge of the Haitian revolution

Mathematical Concepts:

- Polygons

- Angles and their measure

- Supplementary angles

- Parallel and perpendicular lines

Materials and Tools:

- For each group, one Roamer and Roamer World software (from Valiant House, e-mail: info@valiant-technology.com?)

- Map of Haiti

- Rulers

- Sheets of paper for drawing large map

- One computer for each group

Management Procedures:

♦ Arrange desks and chairs to allow space for Roamer 's path on a 4' × 6' map.

♦ Divide students into groups according to the number of Roamers available.

Assessment:

Prior to the study, collect anecdotal records of students' reactions when they encounter a difficult situation. Keep track of the types of questions they ask in completing activities in different subject matters. Administer the pre- and post-tests, and conduct interviews to analyze the students' approaches to problem solving. Have students write reflections on the impact of robotics on their learning. A translated version of the tests should be available for those who might need it. Allow students who are less fluent in writing the option of dictating their responses.

8

SAMAR SARMINI: MUSLIMS AND INHERITANCE PORTIONS

The Muslim Academy is a private school that was established in August of 2000. Student enrollment was 44 the first year, 81 the second year, and 112 for 2003. All of our students have a Muslim background; the majority are from Palestine, and the rest are from Lebanon, Syria, Egypt, Jordan, Sudan, Pakistan, India, South Africa, Haiti, and from the African American population. They come from a middle-class socioeconomic level and are bused from various parts of the city. The majority of the students in the fifth grade are either Palestinian or Jordanian. I enjoyed being a teacher, but as principal it has become possible for me to get to know most of the students. I see it as my duty to provide the best atmosphere in which the children and teachers can prosper. It is a big responsibility and lots of headaches, but well worth the effort.

Samar Sarmini
Principal of the Muslim Academy, New Orleans, LA

Since 2000 Samar Sarmini has been principal of the Muslim Academy in greater New Orleans, LA. Her school of 112 students in grades Pre-K through 6 is small but growing. At first glance there is little to distinguish this school from any other small school. Motivational posters brighten the halls. The curriculum includes the typical academic subjects, plus physical education, art, and computers. The core subjects meet state and local guidelines. Most of the teachers hold or are seeking state certification. Since the school is an extension of the home, parental involvement is encouraged and expected. The students wear school uniforms, and lunchtime brings the smell of pizza.

There are distinct differences, however, that set this school apart. The Muslim Academy strives to foster each child's love of learning and creativity as it reinforces the values, morals, and principles of Islam. The students study

Arabic, Quran, and Islamic Studies. Each day begins with an assembly that consists of physical exercises, prayer, readings from the Quran, and song. Although the Muslim Academy is an equal opportunity school, and open to any student who wants to learn in an Islamic environment, most of the students are Arabs (95%); others are from South Africa, Pakistan, and Haiti. The dress policy specifies that boys and girls wear uniform shirts and pants at all times and requires that girls, beginning in fourth grade, wear a *hijab* (head scarf) and a special, modest outfit appropriate for prayer times. The school calendar aligns with that of the local public schools and includes Muslim holidays. Except for special subjects, for which the students go to another room or an instructor comes to the room, the students are self-contained. The walls of the classroom are decorated with posters—rules for listening, a place value chart, a map of the United States, a model of cursive writing, and a picture of U.S. presidents. Classroom rules include typical entries such as "Follow instructions. Stay seated. Raise your hands." One rule, "Be at your best Islamic behavior," reminds the visitor that this is a special school.

In her role as principal, Samar observes classroom instruction and provides professional development activities for her teachers. Occasionally, she takes over a class and demonstrates a model lesson for the teacher. Samar's own teaching experience includes three years in the elementary and middle grades; and, as a doctoral candidate in Curriculum and Instruction at the University of New Orleans, she is well qualified to mentor her teachers. She taught the lesson described in this profile to Ms. Rana's fifth-grade class. Ms. Rana's class has fifteen students (10 boys and 5 girls), a heterogeneous group with various abilities, learning styles, and achievements. Most of the students are Arab Americans; about half of them speak mostly Arabic at home, and all are bilingual. To discourage mingling of the sexes so that students stay focused on schoolwork, boys sit in the front of the room. Desks are arranged in rows facing the chalkboard at the front of the room.

The fifth graders return from lunch to find Samar and the authors setting up the room for the lesson. They are excited to meet the visitors and to talk about their school. Three of the students have attended the Muslim Academy since its beginning, but most are recent transfers from local public schools. When asked, "How is this school different from the public school?" students are eager to respond. "Our school is only for people who want to learn Muslim," offers Wadi. Nadia agrees, "We study religion here. All of us are Muslims."[1] Ayya adds, "We pray here, and we read Arabic. Before we take a test or begin a lesson we say the *du'a* (prayer)." "We learn Arabic grammar, writing, and reading," Magdi clarifies. "When we go out of our homes and at school," Ehsan responds, "the girls wear scarves." Everybody smiles when Yasser reports, "Except for

---

[1] Not all Arabs are Muslims, and not all Muslims are Arabs.

Fridays when we get pizza, we bring our lunch from home." Jimra wants everybody to know, "There are lots of ways that this school is like the public school. We learn the same subjects, like Math, English, Reading, and PE. And we learn these in English. We have recess, homework, and tests."

ENGAGING STUDENTS

Samar opens the lesson by asking if anyone has lost (in death) a member of the family recently. When Adam responds that his grandmother died, Samar asks, "Do you know anything about her inheritance when she passed away?" Realizing that Adam does not understand the term *inheritance*, Samar clarifies by elaborating.

Samar: You know, her money or property? Did she give anything to her husband when she died?

Adam: I think she had some money.

Samar: Does anyone have an example of when a family member passed away and there was talk of property or money being left to the relatives?

Wadi: My grandpa died.

Samar: Was that your grandpa on your father's side or your mother's side?

Wadi :   My father's side.

Samar: Did your father get any money or land or valuables from your grandpa when he died?

Wadi: I think he got some money.

Having set the context of the lesson with two examples from the students' lives, Samar tells the class, "In today's lesson we're going to use simple cases of inheritance just to get you familiar with the system of Islam."[2] She points to Adam and explains that when his grandmother died, her husband would have taken a definite fraction of her money: "Because there were children, he would take one-fourth of her money, and the children would distribute the rest. If there had been no children, he would have taken half of her money, and the rest of it would depend on other relatives and whoever else was going to inherit from her."

---

[2] The system of Islam classifies inheritors into first class, direct heirs (children, parents, husbands, and wives), and second class, heirs who can have a share of the inheritance in the absence of most of the members of the first class. The two classes may branch into a third one so that grandchildren and their descendants or uncles, nephews, and nieces may also benefit, depending on the circumstances of the descendant. In this way, Islam sees to it that the inheritance is distributed properly when a rich Muslim dies. The reader who wants more information is encouraged to consult the Quran (IV: 11–12).

HISTORICAL BACKGROUND

To establish additional background for the lesson, Samar gives the class some historical background. As she writes on the board the name, "Al-Khwarizmi" both in English and Arabic, she says,

> Al-Khwarizmi[3] lived at the time of the caliph Ma'mun,[4] who asked Al-Khwarizmi to write a book about the different cases of inheritance. Figuring out these inheritance rules takes a lot of thinking—someone taking a quarter of your money, someone else taking one-third, and so forth. It takes a lot of calculation, a lot of math to figure out all these rules. The Muslims wanted to seek more knowledge because of their religion so that they could pray properly and figure out how to get their inheritance. Now in figuring out how to pray properly, Muslims had to figure out the position of the sun. That is how Muslims developed trigonometry—to find the right angles with the sun and so forth.

Returning to the board, Samar writes *"Al-Jabr Wal-Mugabalah"* both in English and in Arabic[5] and continues,

> This is the name of the book written by Al-Khwarizmi. The second half of this book was all about inheritance, cases, fractions, and how to divide up one's property. People who study his book say he was influenced by three civilizations: the Greek, the Mesopotamian, and the Hindu. We are all influenced by other cultures, aren't we? He was able to get elements from each of these cultures to develop the science of algebra.

To be sure that her students are familiar with this branch of mathematics, Samar writes the word *algebra* on the board and asks them if they have heard the term *algebra* before. The students respond in the affirmative. Circling the words *algebra* and *Al-Jabr*, Samar continues the lesson.

---

[3] Al-Khwarizmi was born in what is now Russia in the late 8th century. He wrote several books on mathematics and astronomy. His works introduced the west to decimal notation, the Hindu system of numeration, the science of algebra, graphical solutions to equations, and a map of the known world at his time. He has been called a scientific genius, one of the greatest mathematicians of all time, and the grand master of the golden age of Baghdad.

[4] Al-Ma'mum, a philosopher, theologian, and scholar, lived in the 9th century. He organized at Baghdad an observatory/library, a "house of wisdom." Under his leadership, scholars translated the works of Aristotle, Ptolemy, and others from Greek to Arabic. He is credited for helping bring classical works to Europe during the Dark Ages.

[5] By some translations, Al-Jabr means "transposing a quantity from one side of an equation to another," and Mugabalah means "simplification of the resulting expressions." Others translate the title as the "science of reduction and confrontation" or shorten the title to the "science of equations." The book shows the influences of Hindu and Babylonian methods for solving problems and combines religious law with science in the context of solving Islamic law problems. Practical needs of the people (commerce, lawsuits, legacies, and inheritance) form the basis for the algebraic procedures in the book.

Samar: Do you notice the similarity of the words? Now which of these words do you think came first, the English word or the Arabic word? Let's see what Nadah thinks.

Nadah: I think the Arabic came first.

Samar: The Arabic word came first, and it entered the European culture and became the word for the science of algebra, the science of unknowns—you don't know how much this person is getting in inheritance. The putting together of unknowns is what the science of algebra is all about."

Because the students will be inventing their own algorithms for multiplying fractions in the lesson, Samar next establishes a context for understanding the term *algorithm* with more historical background: "Another contribution of Al-Khwarizmi was the word *algorithm*." Samar writes "algorithm" and provides an example, which she also writes on the board.

Samar: If you want to simplify this fraction $^{12}/_{16}$, what do you do?

Ayya: You divide it by four.

Samar: Why four? Why did you choose four?

Yasser: Four is a common factor.

Returning to the board, Samar writes the equation "$(12 \div 4) / (16 \div 4) = {}^{3}/_{4}$."

Samar: That's your algorithm. You're simplifying the fraction. You found an algorithm to help you do that, and you followed a rule—that's an algorithm. Where do you think the term *algorithm* came from?

She encourages the students to look at the words on the board and does a brief review. The students easily make the connection between Al-Khwarizmi and the word *algorithm*.[6] Samar then finishes establishing the basis of the lesson.

Samar: Today you are going to create your own own algorithm for finding a fraction of a fraction. So, I'm writing this key word, *algorithm*, on the board so that we remember that our lesson is about algorithms.

PROBLEM SOLVING

Next Samar passes out four strips of paper (about 3" × 8") and a page of inheritance tasks (see Figure 8.1) to each student. Together the class reads the first problem that Samar has simplified from the original as it appeared in *Al-Jabr Wal-Muqabalah*.

---

[6] The derivation of the word *algorithm* comes from the Latin pronunciation of Al-Khwarizmi's name as "algorismi." Certain Arabic dialects pronounce the "Kh" sound as "Gh." By some accounts, the word *algorism* is an old word for *arithmetic*.

FIGURE 8.1 INHERITANCE WORD PROBLEMS

---

1. A problem stated in Al-Khwarizmi's book *Al-Jabr Wal-Mugabalah:* A man dies, leaving two sons behind him and bequeathing (leaving) one-third of his capital to a stranger. He leaves ten dirhams of property and a claim of ten dirhams upon one of the sons. What fraction of the man's capital does each son inherit?

2. Nasser dies, and his daughter inherits half of his money. His mother will inherit one-third of the remainder, and his father will inherit two-thirds of the remainder. What fraction will his mother and father inherit out of their son's money?

3. When Nesreen died, she donated one-quarter of her money to the poor. Her father will inherit two-thirds of the remainder, and her mother will inherit one-third of the remainder. What fraction of Nesreen's money will the father inherit?

4. Because the deceased had no children, the deceased's husband inherits two-fourths of her money. The deceased's father will inherit two-thirds of what is left. What fraction of the deceased's money will the father inherit?

5. When Mariam dies, her two daughters inherit two-thirds of her money, her mother one-sixth, and her father the rest.
   a. What fraction of Mariam's money does her father inherit?
   b. If Mariam had $18,000, how much money does her father inherit?

The somewhat puzzled looks on the students' faces prompt Samar to ask, "Does everyone know what the word *capital* means?" Following Ehsan's reply, "Like the capital of Louisiana?" Samar clarifies the term by explaining that in the problem, capital means the man's money, his property, or his inheritance.

Samar: What do we know from the problem?

Wadi: One-third of his capital went to strangers.

Samar: Do you think this is important? If a person dies and says he wants to give one-third of his money to strangers, can you divide up his money before giving the part to strangers? In Islam, you can't. The person gave orders in his will that after he dies, one-third should go to a particular person.

Yasser: The stranger comes and takes the one-third of the money?

Samar: We should give it to him because we honor the wishes of the dead person.

Next, Samar holds up one strip of paper and directs the students to find a way to fold it into three equal parts. Some students immediately find a way, others seek help from a peer, and a few require Samar's assistance to complete the task. After making sure that all of the students have made all of the parts equal, she returns to the problem.

Samar: If the paper represents the capital, how much did the stranger get?

Chorus of students: One-third.

Samar: And what's left if he gives away one-third?

Chorus of students: Two-thirds.

Samar directs the students to use colored pencils to shade in the parts of the paper that are left for the sons. After they color two of the three parts on their papers, she asks them how much they think each of the sons will get from the rest of his money, the remainder. Various answers are offered, but Samar keeps pressing her question. The students eventually realize that each of the sons will get one-half of what is left. She returns to the board and says as she writes, "Each son will get one-half of the money that is left, which is two-thirds, or ½ of ⅔. Now, let's find out the answer." Reminding the students that the part already given away is not a focus right now, she folds back the part of the paper representing the capital given to the stranger and holds up the ⅔ portion. She asks, "Now how should we fold the paper so we can see how much each of the two sons will get?" Jimra holds up his paper and folds it in half lengthwise, prompting Samar to ask if anyone has a different way. Several students fold their papers in half widthwise. "Will the answer be the same if we fold the paper this way?" she asks. Once the students see that the results are the same, she reassures them that both ways are correct.

After everyone's papers are folded, Samar directs the students to shade one of the halves a different color from the previous shading.

Samar: This will represent what one of the sons is getting. This part is half of the two-thirds. Now open the whole paper to see what part of the original capital, what fraction of the father's money, the son is getting. Before you give an answer, look at the whole paper to see how many parts you have in the whole.

While Samar counts aloud with the students, the class realizes that the whole has been cut into six parts.

Samar: So how many parts is the son taking?

Adam: Two.

Using her model, Samar points to the two parts, shaded with two different colors that represent each son's inheritance, and asks another question.

Samar: So what fraction is that?

Chorus of students: Two-sixths.

Samar: Turn your attention to the equation on the board. So one-half of two-thirds equals what?

Rushti: Two-sixths.

Satisfied that her students are not guessing at the answer, but have physical evidence of the amount, she writes, "½ of ⅔ = ²⁄₆" and says, "Now let's do another one."

Ahmed reads the second problem aloud (see Figure 8.1). Samar questions, "What do we know?" As the students volunteer the information from the problem, Samar writes "Daughter gets ½; mother gets ⅓ of the remainder" on the board. Then, as she instructs the students to take a new piece of paper, she asks, "How should we fold this piece?" Most of the students reply, "one-half." Samar directs the students' attention back to the problem and reads aloud the part that supports the choice of one-half. Encouraging her students, she says, "Now that fold is easy, right?" As some students fold the paper in half lengthwise, she asks whether there will be a difference if they fold it another way and says, "Ahmed, try folding it one way, and Yasser, you fold it the other way." Again the students visually see the same results.

Samar: Next, you should color in one of the halves so that you can see the part of the money the daughter is not getting. You might want to write "daughter" on the other part so you remember the part that is given to her. The mother is getting one-third of what?

She presses the students until they tell her that the mother's share is one-third of what is left after the daughter has gotten her part; the mother gets one-third of one-half. Writing "⅓ of ½," she asks them what they are going to do.

Samar: How are you going to fold the half-paper?

Chorus of students: Three.

Samar: How do you know?

Uri: Because the mother got one-third of the half that is left.

The students question which way they should fold next, and Samar again invites them to try both ways. She models a lengthwise fold because it is easier for most of the students to do accurately. She circulates around the room and reminds the students to look at the shaded part of the paper as they decide how much of the money will go to the mother. To the class, she says, "Now change your color and shade in the part the mother is getting. How many of the three parts will that be?" She is pleased by the response, "One part." To make the connection between the problem on the board and the folded paper, she rereads

"⅓ of ½ = ?" as she colors one piece on her model. She then asks, "Now what fraction is this double-shaded part? Let's figure this out."

What has been a very teacher-directed lesson to students sitting in straight rows takes off in a new direction as the students get up out of their seats, cluster together in little groups, fold and unfold as they chat, question each other, and explain their conjectures. Samar circulates among the groups, repeating the question, listening to the discussions, and giving hints where needed. Then she brings the class back to attention.

Samar: So what is ⅓ of ½?

Chorus of students: One-sixth.

Samar: So the equation is ⅓ of ½ = ⅙. And what is the father getting?

Samar directs the students to look at their folded, shaded papers once again as she asks them what is left when the daughter takes her one-half and how much of this half the father is getting. Writing on the board, "⅔ of ½ = ?" she tells the students to shade the parts of the paper that represent the father's share and write "father" on these parts. Unfolding her model paper, Samar asks the students to count along with her as she points to the parts of the paper that go to the daughter, to the mother, and to the father.

Samar: Does everybody see that the father is getting ⅔ of the half that did not go to the daughter, or 2/6 of the whole inheritance?

Wadi: The daughter takes the most, then the father, and then the mother.

Samar: Yes, maybe she is lucky, I guess, that she doesn't have a sister or a brother. If she had a sister or a brother, she would have to share her half.

Waad asks, "Can we do number three?" Pleased by this question, Samar reminds the students that after the next problem, they will be developing the algorithm for multiplying fractions. Before moving on, Samar makes a list on the board of the equations derived from the first two problems:

$$\tfrac{1}{2} \text{ of } \tfrac{2}{3} = \tfrac{2}{6}; \ \tfrac{1}{3} \text{ of } \tfrac{1}{2} = \tfrac{1}{6}; \ \tfrac{2}{3} \text{ of } \tfrac{1}{2} = \tfrac{1}{6}.$$

Nadah reads the third problem (see Figure 8.1). Samar helps students construct the process for a solution similar to the other problems.

Samar notices that Nadia has been quietly folding and unfolding her paper and writing fractions in her notebook. Confident that the shy Nadia has figured out the solution, Samar calls her to the front of the room to explain what she has calculated.

Nadia, who frequently gets eclipsed by her more assertive classmates, timidly steps to the front of the class. Using her paper to demonstrate, she says, "Well, first I folded the paper in four equal parts because that's what the denominator of three-fourths told me to do. Then I turned the paper the other way and folded it in three equal parts because we had to figure two-thirds for the next part of the problem. The denominator this time was three. Then I noticed I had twelve parts when I opened up the paper. So, now I'm figuring out the two-thirds of the three-fourths." Surprising herself that she has said so much in front of the room, Nadia stops abruptly and, holding her head high, walks to the back of the room. The girls give her a "high five" as, smiling, she takes her seat.

Samar thanks Nadia and decides to repeat her steps aloud to the class, adding, "Go back to your whole paper and open it. I want you to tell me how many parts you have in your whole paper." Some students count by inspection; a couple count each part to themselves. In unison she hears, "Twelve." "Now, here is my next question. How many parts is the father getting out of the twelve?" Almost immediately, the response, "Six!" thunders through the room. To the list on the board, Samar writes, "$\frac{2}{3}$ of $\frac{3}{4} = \frac{6}{12}$."

THE ALGORITHM

Samar instructs the students to look at the list of equations on the board (see Figure 8.2) and to justify how they came up with the answers. She tells them to take a few minutes to look at the fraction sentences.

Samar: Look at the results. What is happening? What is going on? We already know that we have the answers because we folded the papers. We tried it, and it works. Now, if I have a fraction of another fraction and I don't have a paper to fold, how can I find my answer?

She pauses before going on, reads aloud the four equations on the board.

**FIGURE 8.2 ORGANIZING BOARD WORK
FOR DISCOVERY OF PATTERNS**

$\frac{1}{2}$ of $\frac{2}{3} = \frac{2}{6}$

$\frac{1}{3}$ of $\frac{1}{2} = \frac{1}{6}$

$\frac{2}{3}$ of $\frac{1}{2} = \frac{2}{6}$

$\frac{2}{3}$ of $\frac{3}{4} = \frac{6}{12}$

Samar: What's going on?"

Abdullah: One times two is two; two times three is six; one times one is one . . ." (Samar interrupts him.)

Samar: Let's try what Abdullah is doing. He seems to be doing some kind of multiplication.

Waddi: Yes. He's multiplying the numerators, and then he's multiplying the bottom numbers.

Eshan: The denominators.

Pointing to the list of equations, Samar and the students continue reading
where Abdullah left off. She presses the students to tell her the algorithm.

Yasser: You trade the fractions. I mean, you switch the second one
upside down." *(He realizes his error and corrects himself.)* Oh, no.
That's division. Here you just multiply.

Samar suggests that they go over Abdullah's algorithm again and asks the
students to explain what the algorithm is.

Ayya: You multiply the numerators together, and you multiply the denominators together. Those numbers are the answer as a fraction.

Samar: Very good, Ayya, but do you think it will work all the time?
Let's pick some problems we have not done and see if that is true. If
we use Abdullah 's algorithm for one-half of two-fourths, what
should be the answer? *(She writes "$\frac{1}{2}$ of $\frac{2}{4}$" on the board.)*

Ayya: Two-eighths.

Samar then asks the students to use paper folding to check it.

Waddi: That works.

Samar: Well, it looks like we do have a nice algorithm that can make
our working with the problems easier. Apply Abdullah's algorithm
to this problem. *(She writes: "$\frac{2}{3}$ of $\frac{3}{5}$ = ?")* What is the answer?

Hands shoot up all over the class. Samar calls on Nadah, who says, "Six-fif-
teenths." Making sure the others know how Nadah got her answer, Samar invites Nadah to the board to point to the numbers she multiplied to get the
numerator and denominator of the answer.

Samar: We can try one more. *(She writes, "$\frac{3}{4} \times \frac{5}{6}$ = ?")*

Magdi: That's easy. That's fifteen over twenty-four.

APPLICATION

Closing the lesson, Samar sums up what the students have accomplished
that day and introduces their next application using fractions.

Samar: Today we figured out how to find the fraction that represents
the part of the inheritance that the mother or father or daughter is
getting. What we will do next time is to find out the value of the
fraction—how much money, for example, that fraction represents.
So, if a person left behind $18,000 and, from problem #2, the father is

taking two-sixths of that amount, we will be figuring out what is two-sixths of $18,000.

Ayya: Can we do it?

Samar: OK. Let's do that one. We'll be using the same algorithm we discovered today. *(She writes on the board, "Son leaves $18,000. Father gets ²/₆.")* How can we start this problem? *(She gets no response.)* There really is a simpler way to solve this problem. Let's start by using a simpler amount, $18, instead of the given, just so we can get a better sense of the problem. What are we now looking for?

Wadi: Two-sixths of eighteen.

Samar: We now have two-sixths of eighteen as our expression. *(She writes "²/₆ of 18" on the board.)* How can we find out what that is?

Wadi: We can divide by six.

Samar: OK. But let's first see if we can use Abdullah's algorithm to solve this equation. *(Samar points to the equation.)* I want to write eighteen as a fraction so that my equation will have two fractions in it just like the ones we did earlier.

Several students: But eighteen is a whole number.

Samar: Yes, but if I want to make it into a fraction, I have to draw a line under it, like this. *(Samar draws a line under "18.")* What is the number I can put under eighteen to make it into a fraction? What number can I use to make eighteen not change in value?

Hearing many suggestions—"zero, six, eighteen, one, twenty"—and sensing her students' confusion, Samar returns to the board and writes, "¹/₁." After establishing that ¹/₁ means the same as 1, she writes, "²/₁." These examples help the students see that a whole number can be expressed as a fraction with a denominator of one and that the value of the whole number will not change.

Continuing, Samar goes back to the equation "²/₆ × ¹⁸/₁" and asks the students what they should do next. "We could multiply two times eighteen and six times one using Abdullah's algorithm," suggests Rushti. Jimra looks puzzled, so Samar goes back to the problems done earlier in class and reminds him how the class got those answers, first from paper folding and then from Abdullah's algorithm.

Mushan: The answer is thirty-six over six.

Nadia: And that's really six.

Samar: So, if the father is getting 6 out of 18 dollars, how many dollars out of the $18,000 is the father really getting?

Chorus of students: Six thousand.

Before the lesson closes, one of the authors, who has been sitting in the back of the room with the girls, notices that Nadah has figured out another way to do the problem and alerts Samar that there is another procedure to share with the class. Samar calls Nadah to the board. Nadah points to the equation "½ of ⅔ = ²⁄₆" and explains, "The two-sixths is really one-third." Acknowledging Nadah's insight, Samar suggests that the class look again at the paper strip from the problem.

Samar: Remember how we counted up the parts that the father received—two out of six? Well, look at the strip in a different way. Can you really see it as three parts instead of six parts? *(Nadah refolds her paper model into three equal parts.)* So we could do the problem using this fraction in lowest terms, too."

Samar ends the lesson by directing the students to write down Abdullah's algorithm in their math journals.

DISCUSSION BETWEEN COLLEAGUES

What is your philosophy of teaching mathematics?

I believe in helping students discover and construct the mathematical concepts rather than providing them with definitions and facts that need to be memorized or accepted as is. I feel that the use of manipulatives is essential in decreasing the abstractness of math. I try to build on students' previous acquired knowledge and attempt to always interrelate mathematical concepts.

How does your being from the same culture enhance your teaching of the students?

I try to tie math with practical aspects of being Muslim; for example, when teaching about the value of time and how much one can do in one minute, I asked students to praise God by repeating a phrase that translates to "there is no God but Allah" and find how many times they can do it within a minute, knowing that with each repetition they gain a reward from God.

What would you do differently if you taught this lesson to students of a different culture?

First of all, I would explain a lot of the basic information that I assume students of my culture already know. I would also explain the importance of religion and its application in the different aspects of a Muslim's daily life. I would also try to relate the Islamic inheritance system to the students' own cultural inheritance for the students to be able to make sense of the lesson as a whole.

Are there any teaching practices that you consistently apply based on the culture of your students?

> When greeting the students in the beginning of the lesson, I always use the traditional Islamic greeting, "Assalamu alaikum," meaning "Peace be unto you." Also, students say a *du'a* (supplication) before they start doing a test as a means of asking for God's support in tough situations, while understanding that hard work and good preparation are essential prerequisites for God's answering their prayers. At this stage, culture is mainly tied with disciplining the students and instilling in them a sense of observance. For example, when they are taking an exam, I remind them that God is aware of their actions and that cheating is prohibited. I then purposefully leave the class for a few minutes to help them practice honesty even with the absence of a teacher.

How do you assess students' participation in classroom discussion?

> I assess discussion not only through the number of questions answered or statements made but also by the quality of these questions and statements. Some students tend to be talkative in class, but they do not really add a lot to the content of the discussions; other students are more conservative and tend to verbalize less often but are more attentive and aware of class events.

How do you assess individual and group performances?

> Group performances are monitored while I am roaming around the class and listening to the interactions of the group members. I later give set of exercises to the individual students so that they may demonstrate their understanding as well as active participation in the overall class activities.

How do you generally assess students?

> Although our lessons incorporate alternative types of assessment, at this point, tests and quizzes are still the main types of formal assessment that we use. We are working towards alternative formal forms for the future.

What are the preferred learning styles of your students? How do you accommodate for these styles?

> The students I have taught all seem to enjoy hands-on work as well as opportunities to share ideas with each other. For this reason, I include these strategies whenever it is feasible to do so.

What recommendations would you make to a teacher who is about to begin teaching in your school?

One of the main recommendations that I always make to a new teacher, especially if she is from a different culture than most of the present teachers, is to expect the possibility of misunderstandings in their daily interactions with other teachers. Often people from the same culture interpret situations differently; hence the probability of misunderstanding is greater when one is dealing with people from other cultures. The best cure for this is be direct about it and to discuss the situation openly with the persons involved or with the principal, if the need arises. Moreover, I always emphasize the spiritual and rewards aspects of this profession as a means of tolerating the hard work it requires.

What are some of the principles of Islam that are reflected in your school?

We encourage self-discipline by prohibiting any kind of inappropriate language or behavior, and we encourage respect toward teachers as well as other students. Making fun of other students in any shape or form is absolutely not tolerated. We also encourage students to be absolutely honest in what they say or do even if that gets them in trouble: it is better to get in trouble in this life than to be punished for dishonesty and lying in the Hereafter. Finally, we try to instill in students the concept of *Taqwa*, being mindful that God is always watching over you.

As the principal of a largely Arab school, your responsibilities, given September 11, are enormous. Can you share with us the effects of that day on you and the students, teachers, school, and community?

Our first reaction was total shock and disbelief. Then, as the news began to sink in, the administration decided to call all of the parents to come to pick up their children from school immediately, for we feared immediate accusations would be made against Arabs and Muslims as was the case with the Oklahoma City bombing. We closed the school for the next few days fearing racial retaliation against the school. Muslim women all over the nation were very cautious about going shopping by themselves for at least a couple of weeks after the incident. One student remembered that a group of non-Arab teenagers who were eating at McDonald's moved to the children's section because the student believed the teenagers "were scared to sit by them." Another student's first thoughts after the September 11 incident were that Americans "will come here to kill us," "will accuse us of doing it," and so "will take us out of the U.S." Most students expressed feelings of sadness about what happened to both planes and buildings.

Here is what may be a difficult question. How do you explain the causes for September 11?

> It is not the Islamic teachings that led to September 11. It is the *interpretation* of these teachings that led to that horrible incident. As educators and practicing Muslims, several of us teachers went over the issue of whether what happened on September 11 was justifiable in Islam or not. The possibility of having any one of our relatives on these planes was very probable. In the U.S., we are not in a state of war, and nothing justifies taking innocent people and using them as a bomb to tear down buildings that stand as symbols of the American economy. What hurt us most was that because the perpetrators were believed to be Muslims, no real mention was made about the few hundred Muslims that died in these crashes because they happened to work at the World Trade Center. It was as though they did not count. The students fully understood that what happened was not backed by the majority of Islamic leaders or by the Muslim community as a whole.

Please clarify what are the Islamic teachings and how they are being misinterpreted.

> I will try to explain as best as I can from my own perspective. Islam requires that we protect each other from aggressive actions, and, if any one Muslim suffers from aggression, then *all* Muslims suffer. We consider it a universal truth that one can retaliate when under attack. Thus, I would fight the enemy to protect my family and myself from an act of aggression—but that is true for anybody. When the U.S. sided with Israel in the agreement that Palestinians leave their homeland and live in tents, that was considered an act of aggression against all Muslims. In the Quran, the *Jihad*, defined as a "holy war," has two facets. The major war is one where we battle against ourselves as we strive to follow the Islamic laws. A second minor war is that of lifting aggression against innocent people. It is the latter definition that is misused to justify acts of violence. Such acts can only be justified if they are against the perpetrators of the aggression. On September 11, my family or I could have been on one of the planes; Arabs, too, died in the World Trade Center; Americans who had nothing to do with any aggression died in those buildings. There is no excuse for that. It is not a holy war when innocent people are targeted.

COMMENTARY

Ethnomathematics is the study of mathematics that values the culture in which mathematics evolved. Urbiatan D'Ambrosio, a founder of the International

Group of Ethnomathematics (IGE), now an affiliate of NCTM, coined the term. IGE aims to elucidate the mathematics of cultures that have been largely ignored or excluded from traditional history in math books so that a more accurate history of mathematics is presented. IGE's belief that rich mathematics is a product of all cultures is evident in the articles and books written by some of its members showing how to infuse the mathematics curriculum with an appreciation for mathematics as a multicultural endeavor (Zaslavsky 1996, 1999; Ascher 1991).

As an example of the exclusion of Arabic/Islamic mathematics, O'Connor and Robertson (2003) write,

> Recent research paints a new picture of the debt that we owe to Arabic/Islamic mathematics. Certainly many of the ideas which were previously thought to have been brilliant new conceptions due to European mathematicians of the sixteenth and eighteenth centuries are now known to have been developed by Arabic/Islamic mathematicians around four centuries earlier. In many respects, the mathematics studied today is far closer in style to that of the Arabic/Islamic contribution than to that of the Greeks (1).

Samar's inclusion of Arabic/Islamic mathematics in this lesson is a fine example of how history can serve as a vehicle for improving self-esteem, as well as an interesting introduction to elementary mathematics. Her students learn that their ancestors were important contributors to mathematics and that they too can engage as mathematicians to discover the algorithm—a word invented by al-Khwarizmi—for multiplying fractions. What is truly a gem in this unit is that the source for developing the algorithm arises out of situations connected not only to the history presented but also to real-world problems still relevant to Muslims today. Thus, history is not used merely as an introduction, but as a vital part of the lesson.

Observations of this lesson show students readily leaving their seats to compare answers with others, busily working on partitioning their "land" to discover patterns, and finally developing the algorithm for the multiplication of fractions. The unit reflects the *Principles and Standards for Numbers and Operations* and adheres closely to research on helping students to build on informal knowledge for understanding multiplication of fractions. In her research, Mack (2001) cites work that supports Samar's pedagogy. Mack lists research that

> proposes that knowledge of partitioning lends itself to understanding the concept of fractions and the various interpretations associated with the concept. One such interpretation is "operator" where a fraction such as "¾" represents a multiplicative size transformation in which a quantity is reduced to three-fourths of its original size by both partitioning and duplicating various portions of the quantity" (269).

For example, once Samar's students interpreted the problem, "⅔ of ¾" as two-thirds of three-quarters of a piece of the land inherited, they then physically reduced the three-quarters' strip of land to two-thirds of its original size through paper folding. In her own research with fifth graders, Mack (2001) reports that this method allows students to build on their informal knowledge to solve problems involving multiplication problems in ways meaningful to them—similar to what occurred with Samar's students.

Samar's persistence in having students find their own rule or algorithm is also to be commended. She easily could have just given the rule and had students complete practice problems. Instead, she had them solve challenging verbal problems that were approachable by all students through paper folding. She then deliberately used the board to organize the results from students' paper folding so that a search for patterns would be fruitful. Interestingly, while many students quickly detected patterns, one of the students, Yasser, called out what he thought was a pattern by saying, "You switch the second upside down." As Samar probed deeper, Yasser, then said, "Oh, no. That's division. Here you just multiply," and he proceeded to show how he agreed with the other students. Did Yasser really detect a pattern from the work shown? Apparently not. In articles about the effect of rules on children's understanding, Behrend (2001) writes, "Teachers often try a quick fix, such as giving a rule to follow. The rule may appear to solve the immediate problem but could actually interfere with students' development of mathematical understanding" (36). It appears that Yasser once learned operations with fractions from a quick-fix approach that was now making it difficult for him to focus on Samar's conceptual approach: He preferred to try to remember those rules rather than to reinvent one quickly and accurately from the class's work.

Samar's approach also shows a respect for students' ways of thinking. She often asked, "Does anyone have a different way for doing it?" Her welcoming of students to the board to show a different approach is only one such example of her view of a classroom as a space to share and enjoy the challenges of thinking. Teachers at all levels sometimes lament that students are not prepared to do the work at hand. Samar demonstrates how students can be kept moving forward in the curriculum while teachers help supply the missing concepts. For example, guided by a student's question, Samar decided to jump to the next day's lesson by introducing an inheritance as money instead of land. In their attempt to solve two-thirds of $18,000, the students' uncertainties prompted Samar first to simplify the problem to an inheritance of only $18 and then to teach the property of dividing a number by one. Once the students understood how to represent eighteen as a fraction, they then solved the problem. Samar's approach to teaching the multiplication of fractions shows that, given appropriate tools and teacher facilitation, students can discover important algorithms.

Both authors enjoyed interacting with students who were so quick to smile and ask questions or ask for help from the authors. Those wishing further information on Arab/Islamic mathematics should check www-gap.dcs.st-and.ac.uk/~history/Indexes/Arabs.html.

CONTACT

Samar Sarmini
Muslim Academy
460 Realty Road
Gretna, LA 70056
Phone: 504-433-1960
Fax: 504-433-1959
E-mail: samarrifai@hotmail.com

UNIT OVERVIEW:
DISCOVERING THE ALGORITHM FOR COMPUTING INHERITANCE PORTIONS

Aim: How can we discover ways to compute inheritance portions?

Objectives: Students will develop their own algorithm for computing inheritance portions requiring multiplication of fractions.

Grade Level: Fifth grade

Number of 60-Minute Periods: One

Source: Mathematics methods books and author's connection to Muslim Inheritance laws

Mathematics Principles and Standards Addressed:

- Principles for equity, curriculum, teaching, learning

- Mathematics as problem-solving, communication, connection, representation

- Number and operation: Understand meanings of operations

Prerequisites:

- Understanding of fractions as parts of unit wholes

- Recognize and generate equivalent forms of commonly used fractions

- Understand various meanings of multiplication

Mathematical Concepts: Using a paper-folding technique and problems of inheritance derived from Islamic law, students develop their own algorithm for multiplication of fractions. They apply their algorithm to solve additional inheritance problems.

Materials and Tools:

- Per student: handout, several pieces of paper about 3" × 8", colored pencils

Management Procedures:

- Have cut paper strips ready for the lesson ahead of time.

- Put students in groups of 2–4.

- Lesson can be taught using direct instruction with problem solving done by students in pairs or small groups.

Assessment:

- Circulate to observe and question students' work

- Homework: Assign practice using the developed algorithm.

9

DIANE CHRISTOPHER: EUROPEAN-AMERICANS AND CULTURES

There is a strong sense of community in my classroom and compassion for others. I like students to work together, to share ideas, to move freely around the room, to do hands-on activities, and to communicate with each other. In this project my students were very self-directed. They learned much about the cultural heritage of their grandparents. They appreciated the cultural differences in our classroom and came to realize that each culture tells a special and unique story.

Diane Christopher
Liverpool Elementary School, Valley City, OH

Diane is a fourth grade teacher at Liverpool Elementary School in the Buckeye School District. A sign declaring Valley City as the "Frog Jumping Capital of Ohio" greets visitors to this quiet mid-west town rich in history. Fertile farmland and salt springs attracted the first settlers, mostly of German descent, to the area about two hundred years ago. Established about one hundred years ago, Liverpool Elementary School educates about 400 children in preschool through sixth grades. In the most recent school year there were two African American students and one Asian American student in the school. The ethnicity of the other students is Euro-American; most trace their ancestors to northern and eastern Europe. Only about 10% of the students receive free or reduced-price lunches. Parental involvement in the school is strong. Many grandparents still live in the local area, and their involvement is commendable.

Each spring fourth grade students in Ohio are required to a take state proficiency exam, the Ohio Proficiency Test (OPT), in mathematics. To prepare for this high-stakes' test, teachers typically "cover" all of the mathematics concepts and terms that the students will meet on the test. In preparation for the OPT,

Diane had already introduced the mathematics topics of this unit to her students, but she was not satisfied:

> I wasn't convinced that my students had deep understanding or could apply their knowledge following this hurried and brief exposure. I wanted to make the topic relevant to the students. That's when I decided to revisit the geometry unit and combine it with our social studies unit on Ohio history in a quilt project.

Diane's twenty-one students (11 girls and 10 boys) are typical of the school's make-up. Two students are identified as gifted/talented; seven students received tutoring in mathematics, and 100% are Euro-American. Until Diane asked her students to find out their ancestors' countries of origin, she assumed they were mostly German, Czechoslovakian, and Polish. To her surprise, the students reported that their ancestors came from thirteen different countries in all. About half of her students have grandparents who occasionally speak a language other than English. Most of the families in Valley City have lived in the area for several generations. According to Diane, the area is undergoing change:

> We have a lot of new families coming here from the city to the country. With a great many people moving into the area, it is a real growing area with a need for new schools. Many longtime residents are fearful of change and of seeing their familiar school building supplanted by larger, more modern buildings constructed outside of the town boundaries.

OVERVIEW OF LESSONS

The unit begins with a review of plane figures (triangle, quadrilateral, pentagon, hexagon, and octagon), lines (intersecting, parallel, perpendicular), kinds of triangles (equilateral, isosceles, scalene), and angles (right, acute, obtuse). Diane uses material from her textbook, and examples from everyday objects to conduct this lesson. To expand the review and to add concepts of similar and congruent figures, and lines of symmetry, as well as to introduce the quilt project, Diane copies examples of quilts from the Internet (e.g., The Decorative Arts Center of Ohio at http://www.decartsohio.org).

ENGAGING THE STUDENTS

Diane: Students, when I say *geometry* what do you think of? Give me some examples of what that word brings to mind.

Hands shoot into the air, and as Diane calls on her students for their ideas, she writes each example on the board under a heading, "Geometry Words."

Keri: I think of figures like rectangles, squares, and triangles.

Brian: Don't forget lines. You wouldn't have shapes without 'em.

Keith: I remember how we studied some weird shapes that had more than four sides, but I don't remember what we called them.

Diane: Would you draw one of these figures on the board for us? Then perhaps someone else in the class can give it a name.

Keith draws a five-sided figure on the board, and eventually Josh remembers that the figure is a pentagon.

Ashley: I guess we should put "circle" on our list even though it isn't made up of straight lines.

Mike: Angles are made of lines. Do we put them on our list?

Diane: Of course, and while we're talking about angles, can anyone give us some examples of kinds of angles?

The class has to stop and think about this for awhile, so Diane draws examples of acute, right, obtuse, and straight angles on the board. Eventually, the names of each are recalled, and each name goes on the growing list. Diane makes sure that each geometric term on the list of required features for the quilt block is reviewed (see Figure 9.1 for guidelines). Next she hands out a copy of the Ohio Star pattern quilt block to each student (see Quilt 1 in Figure 9.2).

Diane: Take a close look at this quilt pattern. Since we've been talking about triangles, let's see if we can find any triangles in this pattern. See if you can find an easy way to count all of the triangles in the pattern.

Chris: Well, I notice that there are repeating parts in this pattern. The corners each have the same shapes, and only the middle seems to be different from the rest of the block.

Diane: Good point. Does anyone notice anything else about the triangles in the pattern?

Morgan: I noticed lots of squares in the pattern. Does that mean we'll have to think of each square as two triangles?

Kim: I think we should only count the actual triangles and not count the squares unless the square has a definite line in it cutting it into two parts.

Before proceeding to another example of a quilt block pattern, Diane asks her students to trace the lines of symmetry in the Ohio Star pattern. Continuing with the discussion of triangles, Diane shows her students a large copy of the Pine Burr pattern (see Quilt 2 in Figure 9.2).

FIGURE 9.1 GUIDELINES FOR QUILT PROJECT: MATHEMATICS

Requirements: You will draw a quilt block to combine research about a country from your family's history with geometry.

Part I: You will need a ruler, a pencil, and a piece of graph paper. Use the ruler and the pencil to make your quilt design on the graph paper. Your design should fill the graph paper. Plan ahead. Your design must include the following:

- At least two different geometric shapes. Choose from these shapes— triangle, quadrilateral, pentagon, hexagon, or octagon. If your quilt has a triangle in it, you must label it as equilateral, isosceles, or scalene.

- At least one example of these lines—intersecting, parallel, perpendicular

- Evidence of a line of symmetry

- One example of an acute angle, or one example of a right angle, or one example of an obtuse angle

Part 2: After you have drawn your quilt block on graph paper, your teacher will make a copy of your block.

- On the copy you should label the geometric shapes, lines, symmetries, and angles listed in part 1.

- On the back of the copy, write three sentences describing the pattern you have created in your quilt block.

- Turn in this labeled copy to your teacher.

- Then use colored pencils to color your quilt block.

Requirements: The research about the country you have chosen must contain information in seven categories. Your written report should cover each of these categories. When you make your oral report, you must include all seven categories. Here are the categories:

1.   Introduction. What is your ancestry? Why did you pick your country? How does your country connect to your family?

2.   What special landmarks and symbols does your country have?

3.   How do the colors you used in your quilt block relate to the country you chose?

4.   Tell about the natural resources of your country.

5.   Tell about the climate of your country.

6.   Include at least three interesting facts about your country.

7.   Write a closing paragraph to conclude your report.

FIGURE 9.2 QUILTS FROM THE DECORATIVE ARTS CENTER OF OHIO

QUILT 1

Ohio Star Pattern

QUILT 2

Pine Burr Pattern

QUILT 3

Shoo-Fly Pattern

From www.decartsohio.org, with permission.

Diane: This pattern is interesting in that it contains examples of all four types of angles that we just reviewed. Let's see if we can spot them, and let's keep a count of the number of each.

The students again notice that this block has repeated patterns in it, and Diane reinforces the idea that large quilts are made by sewing together many blocks so that the finished quilt is really a big example of repeated patterns. Diane has one more sample block for her students to study. It is the Shoo-Fly pattern (see Quilt 3 in Figure 9.2). This time she has a more challenging task for them.

Diane: I'm going to give you a piece of graph paper along with the Shoo-Fly block. This block contains four smaller blocks. I want you to draw a line around one of these small blocks and then copy the quilt one block at a time onto the graph paper. You should use two different colored pencils as you copy the block. That way, you will have an attractive design, and the color will make it easier for you to copy the design.

In this task, Diane's students will apply the concept of symmetries and any terms that did not make the list of "Geometry Words." Throughout these math lessons Diane emphasizes the connection of the activities to the quilt block each of her students will make.

Diane asks her students in their social studies lessons to find out from their parents and/or grandparents what countries their ancestors left to come to America. She encourages them to find out what they can about the immigration of their family members (e.g., when they came to America, where they settled, what work they did).

To get her students thinking about using color and symbols to communicate information about the country that they will portray in their quilt block, she asks the students to review what they know about Ohio by naming a fact about the state to a color.

Diane: We've been studying Ohio history and geography. I want you to think of things that represent Ohio. If you drew these symbols, what color would you use for each symbol?

Mike: Well, I know that people think of Ohio as the Buckeye State, so I'd draw a buckeye and I'd color it brown because that's the color of the buckeye.

Keri: I think the state bird is the cardinal and he's red.

Chris: There's the Ohio flag, and it's red, white, and blue, just like America's flag.

Josh: Can we use blue again? I'm thinking of the Ohio River, and it has to be blue because it's water, and water is blue.

This exercise gets the students thinking about how color and symbols communicate information about a place. When Diane polls the class to find out about her students' ancestors, she finds that thirteen different countries are represented. Many students have ancestors from two or more countries. She tells the students to choose one of these countries and, with an adult's help, to search the Internet and books for information about the country that they picked.

Diane has six computers hooked up to a printer in her classroom, but most of her students will use their families' computers or will be able to complete their research in the school's library during their study time. She gives the students a list of seven required topics to include in their reports. These topics will help the students to focus their research and organize their written and oral reports. (See Figure 9.3 for rubric/guidelines.)

FIGURE 9.3 CHECKLIST FOR QUILT BLOCK PROJECT

Instructions: At the end of the project, each of these items will be checked by your teacher. Be sure that you have checked that you have completed each item before you have them checked by your teacher. Examples that are incorrect will not be checked off as complete.

Part 1: My project contains the following:

1. At least two different geometric shapes

    ___ Triangle (equilateral, isosceles, or scalene)

    ___ Quadrilateral

    ___ Pentagon

    ___ Hexagon

    ___ Octagon

2. At least one example of these lines

    ___ Intersecting

    ___ Parallel

    ___ Perpendicular

3. ___ Evidence of a line of symmetry

4. At least one example of an angle

    ___ Acute angle

    ___ Right angle

    ___ Obtuse angle

FIGURE 9.3 CHECKLIST FOR QUILT BLOCK PROJECT (*CONTINUED*)

Part 2: After you have drawn your quilt block on graph paper, your teacher will make a copy of your block. On the copy you should label the geometric shapes, lines, symmetry, and angles listed in part 1. On the back of the copy, write three sentences describing the pattern you have created in your quilt block. Turn in this labeled copy to your teacher. Then use colored pencils to color your quilt block. Each student is expected to score at the proficient level or above.

Accomplished:

♦ At least 90% of possible geometric figures are labeled.

♦ At least 95% of the geometric shapes are labeled correctly.

♦ At least 95% of the lines are labeled correctly.

♦ At least 95% of the symmetries are labeled correctly.

♦ At least 95% of the angles are labeled correctly.

♦ Paragraph of three sentences accurately and correctly describes pattern; paragraph is free of grammatical and spelling errors.

♦ Quilt block is colored.

Proficient:

♦ At least 80% of possible geometric figures are labeled.

♦ At least 90% of the geometric shapes are labeled correctly.

♦ At least 90% of the lines are labeled correctly.

♦ At least 90% of the symmetries are labeled correctly.

♦ At least 90% of the angles are labeled correctly.

♦ Paragraph of three sentences accurately and correctly describes pattern; paragraph is free of grammatical and spelling errors.

♦ Quilt block is colored.

Unsatisfactory:

♦ Less than 80% of possible geometric figures are labeled.

♦ Less than 90% of the geometric shapes are labeled correctly.

♦ Less than 90% of the lines are labeled correctly.

♦ Less than 90% of the symmetries are labeled correctly.

♦ Less than 90% of the angles are labeled correctly.

♦ Paragraph of three sentences has inaccuracies in the description of the pattern; paragraph has grammatical and spelling errors.

♦ Quilt block is colored.

When the students get the guidelines for making their quilt blocks, they realize that thought, care, and planning will be needed to incorporate both elements of geometry and information about their country into the project. This combination challenges but does not overwhelm the students who eagerly get to work each day. They know that Diane will encourage, advise, and assist, but in the end, the product will be born of their creativity and their personal connection to their family. Each student has personal ownership and a responsibility to the class, too.

For the next three or four days, students busily draw, measure, research, write, color, share ideas, and move around the room to observe each other's work. Two or three students make several rough drafts. The thought of filling up the whole sheet of graph paper with a repeated pattern overwhelms some students, so Diane tells them to think of the graph paper in smaller pieces. Diane later explained her intervention: "I suggested that they fold the paper in four sections and think of the project in smaller pieces because they were having a hard time making the pattern and putting in the geometric shapes in the one big piece."

Not every student finds the project easy to complete. Diane helps two students get started by actually assisting them in making the first row, because one of them is obviously having a hard time figuring out what he needs to do. Some of the students get off-track in coloring their patterns and "mess up," and several others start over more than once.

Once the quilt blocks are finished, both Diane and the students review the checklist to assess their inclusion of the required geometric shapes, transformations, and patterns (see Figure 9.4). Diane holds her students to high standards—They would have to redo the project if the requirements were not met.

Diane uses construction paper to make a border around each block, fastens all the blocks together, and hangs the finished quilt from the ceiling of the classroom. As an incentive, Diane tells them, "On Grandparents' Day, you will give your oral reports to the class and to our visitors."

Excitement fills the classroom as Grandparents' Day approaches and students prepare to give their oral reports. Diane opens a discussion of etiquette, "What are your expectations of your grandparents' behavior as an audience during your presentations?" One student offers, "They'll be good listeners." Diane follows, "How can you tell they'll be listening?" Students' hands fly into the air, "They'll be looking at the speaker." "They won't be talking." "They'll ask questions about the speech at the end." Next, Diane asks, "What will be your grandparents' expectations of the presenters?" Students enumerate, "The presenter speaks loudly and clearly; the speaker shows expression; the speaker talks slowly enough to be understood." Instead of dictating a list of behaviors, Diane helps her students, with her guidance, to form procedures and establish classroom rules.

FIGURE 9.4 SAMPLE STUDENT QUILTS

Grandparents of more than half of Diane's students come to hear their grandchildren's presentations. Diane welcomes them and gives a brief explanation of the project just completed by her students. The students not only report about the country of their ancestors; they also point out the geometric shapes and patterns in their quilt blocks.

FIGURE 9.5 SAMPLE OF STUDENTS' ORAL REPORTS

Ashley: My great-grandparents came from Germany. My block is colored in gold, red, and black for the colors of the German flag. . . . One of the things Berlin is famous for is the Berlin Wall. . . . My block has a hexagon, parallel lines, and acute angles. . . . If you folded my block in half, the shapes would match *(Ashley demonstrates).*

Kristen: I also researched Germany for my project. . . . The green triangles in my block represent the mountains in southern Germany, and this pattern *(she points to alternating squares, triangles and hexagons)* look something like the Brandenberg gate.

Josh (Grinning): And in Germany, they make a lot of beer and sausages.

Jake: My great, great grandpa came from Russia. My block has squares turned like diamonds and acute triangles. . . . It's colored in blue for the flag, red for the Russian army, and green for the hills.

Peter: My great aunt came to America through Ellis Island when she was only 14 years old. She didn't speak a word of English. When she was five, her father came to America to make money so he could send for her in a few years. She was very small when he left her, so she didn't even remember what he looked like. Before she left Poland, he sent her a special pin that she wore on her coat so that her father could recognize her when he met the boat, and she would know him because he had the same pin on his coat. . . . I put a big "P" in my quilt for Poland.

Sam: My great-grandmother came through Ellis Island from Austro-Hungary. When she got to Cleveland she had to cut her hair and wash her clothes in kerosene to get rid of the bugs that she got on the boat. She spoke German when she went to school and got beat up by the kids because it was World War II. She colored eggs at Easter using wax and dye.

Ryan: I've got a good story about my great-grandmother. She came to Cleveland from Rumania. She cleaned houses. When she was walking home one day she tried to cross a flooded stream and had to grab onto a bull to ride him to safety. In my quilt I have the colors of the Rumanian flag and repeated patterns of intersecting lines with those colors.

FIGURE 9.5　SAMPLE OF STUDENTS' ORAL REPORTS (CONTINUED)

Maria:　When my family came from Hungary, they rode in the lowest part of the ship. They changed their name on Ellis Island. Every Easter they went to church to bless the food. My mom still makes the kolache with a nut filling that my grandmother used to make. *(She traces the lines.)* On my quilt I have lots of angles, parallel and perpendicular lines, and lines of symmetry.

Caitlin:　The brown on my quilt is for the soil of Ireland, and the orange and green stand for the flag. My ancestors came to New York and then Cleveland during the potato famine.

Taylor:　I have ancestors from England who came here in 1623. I made patterns of angles and lines in the colors of green, yellow, and red.

David:　My great-grandparents met in England during World War II. They were at a service dance. She was English, and he was an American. I put all three kinds of angles, two kinds of triangles, and lines of symmetry in my quilt, and I used red and blue for the colors of the English flag.

Midway through the time for the reports the students are dismissed to the cafeteria for lunch. Grandparents have brought dishes of their own ethnic foods for their lunch and for the children to sample when they return to class. Diane's room-mother has set a festive table for the platters of galuska, paprikash, kolache, cakes, sweets, and cups of Italian ice. The grandparents delight in tasting, comparing recipes, and recounting how they helped their grandchildren on the project.

Rachael's grandmother:　I had to dig out the family tree to check for names and dates. I found the family crest and other items in the attic.

Sarah's grandmother:　I had to call my sister and my aunt. They have a better memory for this information than I have.

Brandon's grandparents:　We had a fun sharing the past with Brandon. We still make our own spaghetti sauce, Italian ice, and dandelion soup.

Jeff's grandparents (who speak for many):　This was a wonderful project. It got us talking about the past and combined two important school subjects—math and social studies. We wish we could have had such fun when we were in the fourth grade!

Lunchtime passes quickly. When the children return, they are given small portions of the ethnic foods, and then the reports continue. At the conclusion, applause and hugs fill the classroom. It has been a wonderful celebration!

The next day, Diane asks the students to tell what they learned from this project. Students report that they found out something they did not know about another country connected to their family. Some say they were glad they heard stories about their families' past history from their elders. Most students express an interest in learning more about their origin and want to travel to the country they studied. Several students comment on how much they learned about other countries by listening to other students' reports. One student sums up the realization of many, "Our quilt is like the United States. The United States is made up of many different people from many countries just as our quilt is made up of many different blocks. Each block makes the whole quilt beautiful just as each person makes the country beautiful."

Diane closes the unit with a quick review of the math concepts her students applied in the unit. As she asks students to point to examples in the blocks of transformations, shapes, and lines, her students almost jump out of their seats to identify what she is highlighting. All agree that this project was a great way to use geometry and was a lot of fun.

Overall, Diane is satisfied with the efforts of her students, with their application of geometry, and she plans to teach the unit again. She comments, "I had no problems keeping my students on task. This was a very engaging project. I am convinced they were able to apply the geometry ideas we rushed through earlier in the year. What was really interesting is the fact that many students started making patterns in rows as they drew their block. When the block was finished, they were delighted to see more patterns in the block than they had intended. Some patterns ran diagonally as well as up or down, left or right."

DISCUSSION BETWEEN COLLEAGUES

What is your philosophy of teaching mathematics?

> I think math should be engaging and related to daily life. I don't think students see how they can use math in their daily lives. I use a variety of manipulatives in my teaching. I'm a kinesthetic learner, so I know how important the hands-on experiences can be for students. Math is very abstract; it has to be taught so that students can "see it."

What are the preferred learning styles of your students? How do you accommodate for these styles?

> My students love to work together, especially at the end of the school year when they become very social. I try to do auditory, kinesthetic, and lots of visual lessons to accommodate all types of learners in my

class. So even if the method I'm using does not align with the students' strengths, I provide many ways of approaching the subjects I teach and stretch the students' capabilities to learn in many ways.

"Many cultures under one quilt." How did that title come about?

I told the students that we would want to find a name for our quilt and we would brainstorm and share all their ideas. I provided chart paper on which I wrote all their suggestions. We talked about the meaning of the quilt and its connections to math and social studies. From the discussion emerged the idea that even though we are many cultures, we are one class. I wanted the class to see that our quilt would not be beautiful if all the blocks had not come together or if any one block was left out. Each culture has a contribution, brings a special story.

Why did you decide to incorporate this unit into the curriculum?

Well, besides the obvious connection to the Ohio history topics, I welcomed the opportunity to open my students' minds to a multicultural perspective. My school really does not focus on diversity issues, and maybe we should. We are in a region where new people are moving in each week. There can be conflict between the "natives" and the newcomers. I thought that this project would open my students' eyes to the value of diversity and promote acceptance of people who are a little different.

Explain what you do in the lesson in the light of the cultural make-up of your students?

Through the social studies aspect of the unit, I wanted my students to research a country of origin of their ancestors. I gave them a choice. Because I had a diverse population in my classroom, I could not just pick one country for the students to research. I wanted the math and social studies lessons to have a connection to the students, to have meaning to their lives. If I had required that they make their quilt blocks and do their reports about one country, they would not have been able to make a personal connection with the lessons or achieve understanding.

Are there any teaching practices that you consistently apply based on the culture of your students?

I pick local examples to illustrate the concepts in science and social studies that we teach in the fourth grade curriculum. This unit had wonderful tie-ins to Ohio history, a topic in fourth grade social studies. As far as teaching practices go, I hold my students to high standards and push each student to reach his/her potential. I really do believe that all students can learn and see my job as making learning happen for all. For me, their culture is the sum total of all the variables that make up their world-view (gender, race/ethnicity, religion, exceptionalities, etc.). The world-view of my students is shaped by their ethnicity, their small-town world, their family values, etc. So for me, it is important to know who they are and make my teaching relevant to their lives. This project really gave me new insights into each student's world-view.

What would you keep and/or change the next time you teach this lesson?

I would ask the students to make their quilt block even more particular to their own family background. Some of the students asked their grandparents for specific information about how they came to this country. I would encourage more of that conversation and look for special family stories or symbols to be incorporated into the quilt. Wouldn't that be a wonderful way to bridge the generations and make the project even more engaging for the children?

What would you do differently if you taught this lesson to students of a different culture?

Most of what I did would not be different at all. I would still give the students a choice of the country to research and incorporate the same math concepts. Because of the varied learning approaches in the unit, student learning styles would not pose a problem. Because there is so much choice and the lesson is so open, it is transportable to any setting—a large city school, a rural school, and so forth.

How do you generally assess students?

I use a variety of assessments—observations, questioning, written tests. When I use tests from the teacher's manual, I adapt them by shortening them, changing items to fit my students and the way I teach the lesson, or eliminating some items all together. Sometimes I ask proficiency-type questions on each unit test. I share the rubric for grading 2- and 4-point questions so that they can see how the questions will be graded. I ask them to grade sample questions according to the rubric so that they can understand better how to answer those types of questions when it really counts. Then I have them self-evaluate their own work.

What recommendations would you make to a teacher who is about to begin teaching in your school?

Most of the teachers at Liverpool Elementary School have taught in the building for a long time. Many were born and raised in the local area. In the past, teachers coming here from other parts of the state or from other parts of the country would have had a harder time fitting into the school and would have had to prove themselves. Nowadays, a teacher's qualifications and his/her ability to do a good job for the children are looked at when someone is hired. A new teacher would be watched to see if he/she meets the high expectations of the community. Our community wants the very best teachers for its children and likes it when someone from the area returns to teach in the local school. I suspect this is the reality in many midwestern towns.

COMMENTARY

What makes Diane such an effective teacher of mathematics? According to the *Principles and Standards for School Mathematics* (2000),

> Teachers establish and nurture an environment conducive to learning mathematics through the decisions they make, the conversations they orchestrate, and the physical setting they create. . . . In effective teaching, worthwhile mathematical tasks are used to . . . engage and challenge students intellectually. Well-chosen tasks can pique students' curiosity and draw them into mathematics (18).

One way that Diane draws her students into mathematics is to integrate mathematics into the whole curriculum. In this unit she combines social studies, language arts, visual arts, and research experiences for her students. While she gives them guidelines, students decide what the final product of their efforts will look like and whether the outcome meets the high standards that she *and* they have set for their work. Students' communication of their mathematical ideas is paramount for Diane: "I have to be sure my students can explain their mathematics understandings to me and to their peers. I do not rely on classroom or state test scores as the only measures of whether or not a student knows the mathematical concepts."

Does Diane teach in a multicultural classroom? At first glance, the students in her classroom appear to have similar physical characteristics, and one could assume they are all of one culture. As Diane puts it, "It's interesting to note that on the surface no one could have picked out the students' background. Their culture was not obvious by looking at their skin tones, hair color, speech patterns, and so forth. I was amazed at how many different nationalities are represented in my classroom." Under the assumption that all her students were "the same," she lumped all her students into one homogeneous group by ethnicity, then assumed common characteristics, and taught accordingly. What she found when she dug a little deeper is a richness of family background that she could use in making her mathematics lessons more personal to each student's family.

What is important in this chapter is that a group of students who, on the surface, seem to be all the same, have very different ethnic origins, different cultures. On the surface, Diane's classroom could probably be considered monoethnic. However, what could be easily overlooked is that everyone belongs to more than one microculture, so even in a "homogeneous" classroom, there are still many cultures represented. Regardless of the setting, therefore, teachers must teach with a multicultural perspective (Davidman and Davidman 1994).

What is a multicultural perspective? According to Bennett (1999), multicultural education in the United States is an approach to teaching and learning that is based upon democratic values and beliefs and affirms cultural pluralism. By its very origins, the United States is exceptionally rich in the cultural groups that compose the nation and the value we place on the contributions of the many peoples who live here. Davidman and Davidman (1994) maintain that, "a multicultural perspective is a state of mind, a way of seeing and learning that is shaped by beliefs about multiculturalism in American history and culture . . . [that] helps teachers see that culture . . . [is a] potentially powerful variable in the learning process of individuals and groups" (7). These beliefs help teachers maximize the learning experiences of each individual student in their classrooms, incorporate the contributions of many cultural groups, help students use their cultural resources to develop their skills and to explore the subject matter, and instill core values of acceptance and appreciation of diversity (Hernandez 2001).

How does Diane teach with a multicultural perspective? She not only reinforce mathematical concepts in this quilt unit, but also taught her students core American values: to embrace diversity, to respect ancestors and to recognize the dignity of each person. Through this unit, Diane, too, gained a new appreciation for the uniqueness of each of her students. She and her students discovered commonalties as well as differences about each other as they studied each other's country of origin. According to Diane,

> My students learned that many of them had similar cultural backgrounds and connected with each other through that. They also appreciated their differences. I think that maybe for my students to appreciate the cultural differences among themselves they first had to learn about and to value their own culture.

Since many European-American students feel that they do not have a culture in the same sense as more culturally identifiable people do (Nieto 1996), teachers must orchestrate experiences for these students to identify and to celebrate their own cultures so as to subsequently celebrate all cultures (Sharp 1999).

Appreciation for Diane's unit extended outside of the school to the student's families. Grandparents attending the students' presentation were happy to help with stories from the "old countries" to incorporate in the quilt. The fact that *their* story was important to the current generation of students must have made some positive impact on their view of schooling today. In Diane's words,

> Given that the community is undergoing unsettling changes, I have to wonder if the quilt stories depicting sudden and drastic changes in the lives of the immigrant might not have also served as a reminder to the community that change, after all, is not that bad.

CONTACT

Diane Christopher
Liverpool Elementary
3140 Columbia Road
Medina, OH 44256
Phone: 330-722-8257
Fax: 330-725-0164
E-mail: dchristopher@buckeyeschools.org

UNIT OVERVIEW:
MANY CULTURES UNDER ONE QUILT

Aim: How can we apply geometric concepts to make quilt blocks of our heritage?

Objectives: Students will explore polygons, triangles, and similar and congruent figures. Students will identify different types of line segments and explore quadrilaterals and line symmetry.

Grade Levels: Fourth and fifth grades

Number of 60-Minute Periods: Seven Math periods and five Social Studies periods

Source: Teacher-created concept; The Decorative Arts Center of Ohio: *Geometric Design in Ohio Quilts* (http://www.decartsohio.org)

Mathematics Principles and Standards Addressed:

- Principles for equity, curriculum, teaching, learning, technology
- Mathematics as problem solving, communication, connection, representation
- Algebra: Understand patterns, relations, and functions.
- Geometry: Analyze characteristics and properties of two-dimensional figures. Apply transformations and use symmetry to analyze mathematical situations. Use visualization, spatial reasoning, and geometric modeling.
- Measurement: Apply appropriate techniques, tools, and formulas to determine measurements.

Prerequisites:

- Recognition of common polygons, parallel and perpendicular lines, types of triangles (by sides and angles)
- Use of a ruler and graph paper
- Recognition of similar and congruent figures, geometric transformations of translation, rotation, and reflection
- Formation of geometric patterns, particularly along a line of symmetry

Mathematical Concepts: Students apply their knowledge of geometry to design and produce a quilt block illustrating their research about their family's country of origin. Students explore congruent figures, symmetries, and transformations of translation, rotation, and reflection.

Materials and Tools:

♦ Per student: ruler, graph paper, assorted colored pencils and markers, construction paper, Internet access

♦ Per class: Samples of quilts

Management Procedures:

♦ Prepare sample quilt blocks consisting of a variety of geometric figures and relationships for students to analyze.

♦ Engage parents to assist students with research on the family's ethnicity.

♦ Provide time in the school day for students to use the Internet for research.

Assessment: Circulate to observe and question students' work. Use rubric to assess students' identification of geometric shapes and relationships.

10

CHARLENE BECKMANN, KARA ROZANSKI, AND TARA PLUMMER: A THREE-WAY SCHOOL/UNIVERSITY COLLABORATION: THE TORTOISE AND THE HARE

Teaching middle school mathematics is a challenge in itself. The activities in this chapter met this challenge by immersing students in engaging activities that built their intuition about linear functions through conceptually developing their understanding of slope and y-intercept in the context of motion over time.

Charlene Beckmann
Kara Rozanski
Tara Plummer

Dr. Charlene Beckmann (Char), a university mathematics and mathematics education professor first met Tara, a secondary teacher, and Kara, an elementary teacher, while they were undergraduates enrolled in her mathematics and mathematics education courses. Both teachers struck Char as "perceptive and insightful" mathematics teachers. In these courses, Char provided students the opportunity to experiment with a motion detector and a Calculator-Based Laboratory (CBL) attached to a graphing calculator. The unit described here was inspired by Kara's response to a journal assignment after having experience with CBLs and motion detectors. Kara and Char expanded the activity and then asked Tara to join them in piloting it with middle-grade students. Char invited both teachers to join her in cowriting this and other articles. The teachers eagerly accepted, and a three-way school/university collaboration was born.

Aesop's fable *The Tortoise and the Hare* provided the setting from which to develop students' conceptual understanding of linear functions, particularly the concepts of slope and *y*-intercept.

"How do I get students, no matter what their level, to understand the concept of slope?" This is a common question and one that Char, Kara, and Tara all asked during the creation and piloting of *The Tortoise and the Hare* activities. The idea of slope can be a complicated one for students to understand and for teachers to explain. It is one thing to teach students the mechanics of finding the slope, but it is entirely another to help students attach meaning to slope in the various contexts in which it arises.

The class with which the activities were implemented and whose students' responses are described in this profile was Tara's eighth grade class. Char, Kara, and Tara used the Transition Mathematics program from the University of Chicago as their base. Students in this class were accustomed to having prospective teachers from Char's university class in their classroom on a weekly basis. So having a college professor join the class for a week seemed natural to the students.

PREPARATORY ACTIVITIES

Some preparation was necessary before beginning this activity in the classroom. Throughout the year, Tara provided students many hands-on learning opportunities. Students had participated in many weeks of team building and got along as a class very well. They were used to working with a partner or in small groups on a daily basis, but they could also be productive when asked to work individually. As for the content, Tara made sure students had a good understanding of the Cartesian coordinate plane, were able to compile tables or t-charts, and were able to solve an equation in the form of $ax + b = c$. She also introduced them to the graphing calculator and the calculator-based ranger (CBR).

ENGAGING STUDENTS

DAY 1: RUNNERS TAKE YOUR MARK

Throughout the year, Tara begins each class asking for a recap of the prior day's events. Before beginning *The Tortoise and the Hare*, she asks the students to recall the previous day's events with the CBR (a motion detector attached to a graphing calculator). The students had spent the prior day duplicating various graphs using a CBR to graph their walking. They experimented with different walking rates, starting points, and directions. They created simple linear graphs first, then absolute value functions, and finally a step function.

FIGURE 10.1 CAN YOU WALK THESE GRAPHS?

Using the graphing calculator and a CBR (calculator-based ranger), see if you and your classmates can create the following graphs:

1.

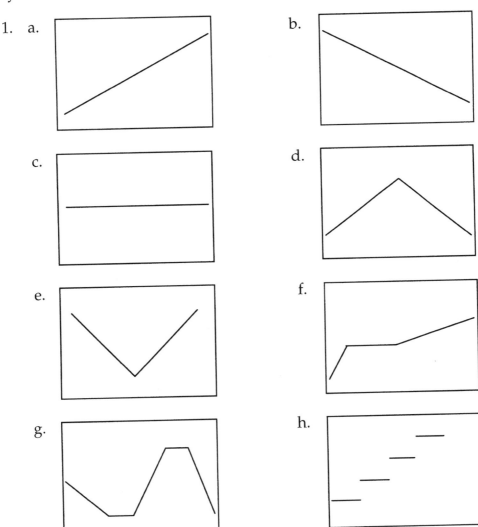

2. Challenge each other to walk various graphs. Draw them on paper and have your group members try to match them on the graphing calculator. Try to graph curves too!

The students were not aware of the names of the graphs they were creating; they were just walking to discover how to create graphs made up of straight-line segments. They also experimented with different starting points, directions, and speeds. Discussion focused on how the students made the different graphs, with special emphasis on how to create different steepnesses. Tara begins her review by asking review questions based on Figure 10.1:

Tara: How do you determine where to start walking for each graph?

Marie: Start close to the motion detector and walk away from it when the graph is going up, and do the opposite when the graph is going down.

Tara referred to the absolute value graph students walked.

Tara: The graph that most of you walked that is on your calculators has a round top. How can we make it more like an angle?

Mimi: To make a sharper corner, change directions quickly.

Tara: OK. Now, how can we make an absolute value graph? And how can we be sure that the steepness is the same in both directions as in graphs d and e?

James: To make the absolute value graphs, keep the same pace as you walk forward and backward.

Tara: Who can show us how to make the step function graph shown in graph h?

To this question Brandon, Tony, Justin, and Joe immediately get up to demonstrate. They stand in a single-file line in front of the CBR and jump out of the range of the motion detector at certain time intervals. At first, Marie asks, "What are they doing?" Tomeca replies, "I don't know, but that's not going to work." But after seeing that the solution is correct, they nod their heads in agreement saying things like "OK, that makes sense" and "Oh, I get it." Tara asks, "Can you explain what you understand now?" "Well," Tomeca says, "whenever one of them jumps out, then the motion detector picks up the next person standing further away. That's why we see those steps."

After the recap of the CBR activity, Tara feels ready to launch the challenging problem for the unit. She begins by asking one of the students to read Aesop's fable of *The Tortoise and the Hare*:

> *The Hare was once boasting of his speed before the other animals. "I have never yet been beaten," said he, "when I put forth my full speed. I challenge anyone here to race with me."*
>
> *The Tortoise said quietly, "I accept your challenge."*
>
> *"That is a good joke," said the Hare. "I could dance round you all the way."*
>
> *"Keep your boasting till you've beaten," answered the Tortoise. "Shall we race?"*
>
> *So a course was fixed and a start was made. The Hare darted almost out of sight at once, but soon stopped and, to show his contempt for the Tortoise, lay down to have a nap.*

The Tortoise plodded on and plodded on, and when the Hare awoke from his nap, he saw the Tortoise nearing the winning post, and could not run up in time to save the race. Then said the Tortoise,

"Plodding wins the race."

"What do those last words mean?" Tara asks. Tiffany replies, "That if you just keep at it, you'll win." Tara asks, "Can anyone tell us a bit about Aesop?" The students vaguely remember having heard Aesop's name, so Tara adds, "Aesop was a Greek philosopher who lived in the 6th century BC. He wrote hundreds of tales like this. They are called fables, and each has a moral. If you search for Aesop on the web, you will find over 600 of his fables."

Tara next distributes the handout, *Runners Take you Mark* (Figure 10.2) that requires students to compare the movement of the Tortoise, who always plods at the same steady rate, to that of the Hare, whose rate, though constant over intervals, is less consistent. The students are presented a variety of scenarios to compare, some with positive and some with negative slopes. In all of the scenarios, the students build intuition for the concepts of slope and linear functions without actually finding values for slopes. As a result of this activity, the students are able to talk intelligently about the relationship between the relative steepness of two linear graphs and the relative speeds of the characters each represents.

Tara: How can we determine which animal is moving the fastest from a graph?

Jessie: By the steepness of the graph.

Tara: Tell me more. How does the steepness do that?

Marie: The Hare's graph is steeper than the Tortoise's when the Hare is moving faster.

The next step in *Runners Take Your Mark* is to graph the motion of each of the characters throughout the race. This is done as a whole-class activity. Tara asks the students what to graph, and she displays what they tell her to draw on a white board with the Cartesian plane displayed in the front of the classroom. After the axes are labeled, Tara asks the class how to draw the Tortoise's graph. Tim responds, "Draw a straight line from corner to corner." Tara then names a line, $y = W$, where W is a constant, as the winning line before graphing the Hare's run.

Tara: Let's list some of the properties of the Hare's graph.

Ryan: The Hare's graph needs a flat part in the middle for when he's taking his nap.

Jessie: When the Hare wakes up and runs again, his graph has to be steep.

Justin: The graph crosses $y = W$ after the Tortoise's graph did.

FIGURE 10.2   RUNNERS TAKE YOUR MARK *(WITH SOLUTIONS)*

---

1. a. On the same axes, sketch possible distance versus time graphs for the
       Tortoise and the Hare, where the horizontal axis (x-axis) represents time
       and the vertical axis (y-axis) represents distance.

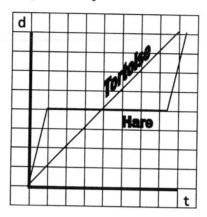

   b. For the intervals over which both the Tortoise and the Hare are
      moving, how can you tell from the graph which animal is moving
      faster? *The graph is steeper for the faster animal.* Why does your answer
      make sense? *More distance is covered in the same amount of time by the
      steeper graph.*

2. The Hare is embarrassed by the results of his race with the Tortoise and de-
    mands a rematch. Suppose the Tortoise plods along at a slow but constant
    pace, and the Hare travels as described below. On the same axes, sketch
    possible graphs for the Tortoise and the Hare for each of the following sce-
    narios. Let $y = 0$ indicate the starting point of the race and $y = W$ indicate
    the winning post. In each case, write a sentence or two to explain why you
    drew the graphs as you did.

   a. The Tortoise and the Hare start the race at the same time and place, and
      the Hare keeps hopping at a constant rate. *The Hare moves much more
      rapidly than the Tortoise, but still at a constant rate. The Hare's graph is steeper
      and reaches the winning post first.*

   b. The Hare is basically lazy, so he plans his strategy to sleep at the starting
      line as long as he can and begins to move in just enough time to finish
      the race a few seconds ahead of the Tortoise. The Tortoise starts the race
      without the Hare. *The Hare starts at a later time, so his starting point has a
      larger x value but the same y value. His graph is steeper, but still linear, and he
      arrives at the winning post just before the Tortoise.*

   c. Create your own Hare scenario. Write the story. Sketch the graphs for the
      Tortoise and the Hare on the same axes. *Answers will vary.*

FIGURE 10.2   RUNNERS TAKE YOUR MARK (CONTINUED)

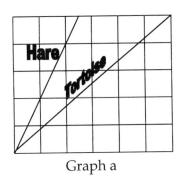

Graph a

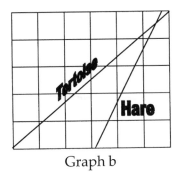

Graph b

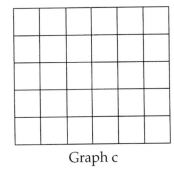

Graph c

3. The graphs below show the travels of the Tortoise and the Hare between the starting line and the winning post where $x = 0$ indicates the starting time for their travel, and $y = 0$ indicates the starting line of the original race. For each of the following, explain how you know your answers are correct.

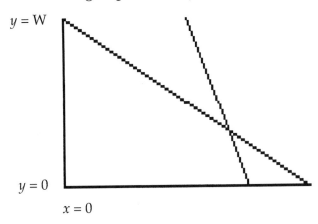

a. From where are they traveling? To where? *From the winning post to the starting line. The Tortoise plods at a constant steady pace, so his is the graph with the less steep slope. Both characters start at y = W, the winning post, and end at y = 0, the starting line.*

b. Who left first? *The Tortoise's graph began at x = 0, the Hare's graph doesn't start until later, so the Tortoise left first.*

c. Who arrived first? *The Hare reaches y = 0 at an earlier time than the Tortoise, so the Hare arrives first.*

4. Suppose the Tortoise's initial race toward the winning post looks like the graph below where each tick mark on the *x*-axis represents one minute. If the Tortoise had started at a different place or time or had run at a different speed, the resulting graphs would be similar but not the same. On the same set of axes, sketch graphs that show the following scenarios, and write a sentence for each explaining how you know your new Tortoise graph is correct.

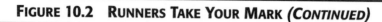

FIGURE 10.2   RUNNERS TAKE YOUR MARK *(CONTINUED)*

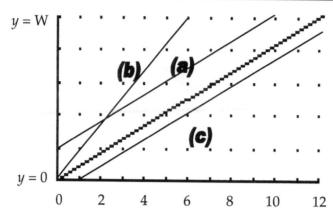

a. The Tortoise started the race at a point one-fifth of the way to the winning post and plodded at the usual speed. Label this graph (a). *The graph must start at the first tick mark on the y-axis. The speed is the same, so the slope will be the same.*

b. The Tortoise started the race at the starting line but plodded at a rate twice as fast as in the original race. Label this graph (b). *The Tortoise will reach the winning post at 6 minutes instead of 12 minutes because he is traveling twice as fast.*

c. One minute after the starting gun fired, the Tortoise began the race at the starting line plodding at the usual speed. Label this graph (c). *The Tortoise starts at x = 1 and travels at the same speed, thus having the same slope.*

d. In which of these scenarios would the Tortoise finish in the least amount of time? How do you know? *Scenario b because its line is steeper.*

5. On another set of axes, draw a pair of lines that are neither vertical nor horizontal. Name your characters and write a travel story about your characters that is consistent with your graphs. *Answers will vary.*

Tara then reads through a series of racing scenarios between the Tortoise and the Hare for which students are to draw the graphs and write a few sentences explaining how the graphs pertain to the scenario (see question 2, Figure 10.2). Working with partners, the students work through the graphs and sentences about the first two scenarios with ease (parts 2a and 2b). They begin creating their own scenarios for the racers in class (part 2c). Before class ends, Tara asks the students to share their stories aloud. One of the more creative stories follows:

The Tortoise put sleeping powder in the Hare's drink. So the Hare takes off, and before the finish line he falls asleep. The Tortoise comes and eats the Hare, and because he ate too much, he dies. So the Tortoise would have won.

Questions 4 and 5 of Figure 10.2 are assigned for homework. In question 4, students are to compare the Tortoise's actual motion with several alternative scenarios, graphically and in words. In question 5, students are to create their own characters and race scenario, graphically and in writing.

DAY 2: THE TRODDING TORTOISE

The second day begins with a review of *Runners Take Your Mark*, which required students to draw graphs of different race scenarios for the Tortoise (see question 4 in Figure 10.2). Tara displays the graph in question 4 on the overhead. The following conversation ensues:

Tara: How fast is the Tortoise going in part a?

Santana: The same as before.

Tara: So how should the graph look?

Santana: The same steepness.

Tara: Will the graph start in the same place?

Ryan: No, the Tortoise started closer to the winning post.

Tara: How can we show that on the graph?

Ryan: Since it's one-fifth of the way, go up one tick mark on the *y*-axis.

Tara: For part b, how can we change the graph to show the Tortoise is going twice as fast?

Mimi: The line will be steeper.

Tara: How steep?

Mimi: Twice as steep as the original.

Tara: For part c, what changes do we need to make on the graph?

James: He started at one minute.

Tara: So how can we show that on the graph?

Joe: Shouldn't it start at one minute and go up the same as the other graph?

Tara: Class, what do you think of Joe's idea?

Kristen: I agree!

Alecia: He's still going the same speed, so the graph is the same steepness. He's just starting later.

As the students answer the questions, the graphs are drawn on the overhead. To answer question 4d, the students look at the graphs and notice that the graph in part 4b reaches the winning post in the shortest amount of time.

Both correct responses and misconceptions are found in the homework that the students turned in for question 5. See Figure 10.3 for a sample story written by Kelly.

FIGURE 10.3 KELLY'S STORY

Two girls went for a walk. They wanted to see who could get back to the house fastest. Girl #1 started off faster than Girl #2. Soon Girl #2 got tired and rested. At about the same time, Girl #1 got tired too. After some time, Girl #2 decided to run as fast as she could, but she got tired again, so she rested. Girl #1 woke up and decided to run at a constant speed the rest of the way. Girl #2 woke up and ran too, but Girl #1 beat her.

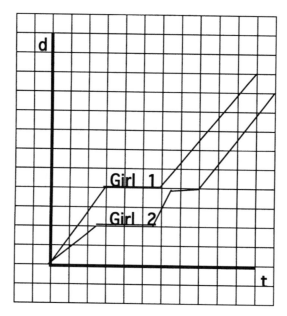

Kelly's story shows Tara and Char that some students are starting to understand the connections between steepness and speed and that the horizontal sections of the graph show the character is resting. But some students turned in work that shows misconceptions. For example, one student drew a graph resembling nearly vertical zigzags and wrote a story about an animal climbing up and down a range of mountains. Others simply wrote the story of *The Tortoise and the Hare* and merely changed the characters' names. A cursory review of students' work leads Tara and Char to give more examples and to keep working to help the students acquire an understanding such concepts as constant rate, zero rate, and change in direction versus accumulated distance.

After collecting the homework, Tara starts the class working on *The Trodding Tortoise* activity (Figure 10.4) in which the students use information about the speed of the Tortoise to complete a table, plot a graph from the table, and find the equation of a linear function to fit the data and the graph. In this first experience with finding an equation of a linear function, the *y*-intercept is zero. Slope is defined with students realizing that the slope of the line is the same as the speed and also the same as the coefficient of *x* in the equation of a linear function.

FIGURE 10.4 THE TRODDING TORTOISE

During the initial race between the Tortoise and the Hare, the Fox recorded the speed at which both the Tortoise and the Hare were traveling. The Fox observed that the Tortoise plodded along at a rate of 20 meters per minute throughout the 1000-meter race.

1. Complete the table below indicating the distance traveled by the Tortoise in the time elapsed.

Time elapsed in minutes	0	1	5	10	11	15	25	...	x
Distance traveled in meters	0								

2. Using the information in the table, sketch a graph showing the Tortoise's progress.

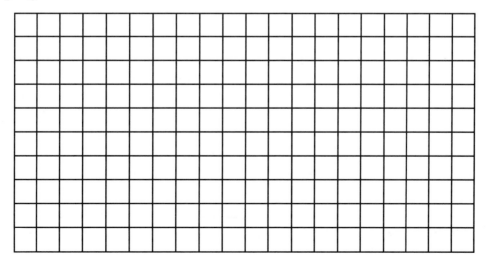

FIGURE 10.4 THE TRODDING TORTOISE (CONTINUED)
---

3. a. In one minute (*x*), how far did the Tortoise travel (*y*)?

    b. What was the Tortoise's speed for this race? Label the units.

4. How can you find the distance that the Tortoise traveled directly from the number of minutes that have elapsed since the start of the race?

5. a. If *x* is the time elapsed in minutes and *y* indicates the distance the Tortoise traveled in meters, write an equation showing the relationship between *x* and *y*. $y =$ _____

    Test the equation with values from the table.

    b. How does the answer to (3b) relate to the equation found in (5a)?

    c. How long did it take the Tortoise to complete the race?

6. The *slope* of a line is defined as the change in *y* divided by the change in *x*. When *y* increases as *x* increases, the slope is positive. When *y* decreases as *x* increases, the slope is negative.

    Complete the table below for the Tortoise's travels for each of the time intervals indicated.

Time Interval	Change in x	Change in y	Slope of the Tortoise's Graph	Tortoise's Speed
0 to 5 minutes				
5 to 10 minutes				
10 to 20 minutes				

Tara distributes *The Trodding Tortoise* handout and asks the students to follow along as she reads the details of the Tortoise's race to them. While finding distances corresponding with various travel times for the Tortoise (see the table in problem 1 of Figure 10.4), the students have an easy time finding the recursive relationship relating subsequent distances traveled, but they have a hard time finding the explicit formula relating distance to elapsed time. For example, Brandon determines that the Tortoise traveled 100 meters in 5 minutes, 200 meters in 10 minutes, and 300 meters in 15 minutes. He can extend the pattern for distances for subsequent 5-minute time intervals. However, Brandon is unable to find an equation that will tell him the distance traveled directly from any give time.

To help the students see the importance of the relationship between distance and time, Tara says, "Let's include 1 minute and 11 minutes in the table." With these changes now reflected in the table (see problem 1 in Figure 10.4), Tara continues to ask questions to guide the class toward a focus on the relationship between distance and time.

Tara: What distance did the Tortoise travel in 1 minute? 11 minutes? How do you know?

Brandon: In 1 minute the Tortoise goes 20 meters because his rate is 20 meters per minute. For 11 minutes I can add how far the Tortoise goes in 1 minute to how far he goes in 10 minutes, so he goes 20 + 200 meters or 220 meters in 11 minutes.

Huey: Or we can just multiply the number of minutes by 20 meters per minute to get how far he goes.

The students are assigned the last table (see problem 6 in Figure 10.4) as homework.

DAY 3: THE HOPPING HARE

Tara begins class by checking students' understanding of slope.

Tara: How did you find slope to fill in the table in problem 6 of Figure 10.4?

Kelly: Divide the change in y by the change in x.

Tara: So let's go through the table.

Tara displays a copy of the table on the overhead and calls on students at random to fill it in. After the table is complete, the students notice that the speed of the Tortoise and the slope are always the same.

Tara: Were you surprised that the slope and speed are the same?

Tim: At first I was, but then I realized that the change in y is the change in distance and the change in x is the change in time, so the slope is just the speed the Tortoise traveled.

Tara: Wow! I'm impressed, great answer!

In *The Hopping Hare* (Figure 10.5), the students examine the Hare's race more closely. They use information about the speed of the Hare to complete a table. They plot a graph of a piecewise linear function from the table and find the equation of a linear function to fit the data for the first two minutes of the Hare's travel. They also determine that for the portion of the race when the Hare is sleeping, the slope of the graph and the Hare's speed are zero. This activity provides more practice for students to find slopes and relate them to speed.

FIGURE 10.5 THE HOPPING HARE

The Fox made the following observations about the Hare's behavior during the initial race between the Tortoise and the Hare:

    I. The Hare traveled at a constant rate of 250 meters per minute for the first two minutes.

    II. The Hare's nap was exactly 47.5 minutes long.

    III. The Hare woke with a start and then ran the last part of the race at a constant rate of 500 meters per minute.

1. a. Complete the following table indicating the distance traveled by the Hare in the time elapsed.

Time elapsed in minutes	0	0.5	1.0	1.5	2.0	2.5	x, for x between 3 and 49.5 minutes	49.5	50	50.5
Distance traveled in meters										

    b. Sketch a graph showing the Hare's progress from the information in the table.

2. Complete the following table for the Hare's travels for each of the time intervals indicated:

Time Interval	Change in x	Change in y	Slope of the Hare's Graph	Hare's Speed
0 to 5 minutes				
5 to 10 minutes				
10 to 20 minutes				

FIGURE 10.5 THE HOPPING HARE (CONTINUED)

---

3. Write an equation relating elapsed time and distance traveled for the Hare's first two minutes of travel. $y =$ _____ Test the equation with values from the table.

4. Answer the following questions using the equation you found for (3).

5. a. How far did the Hare travel during the first 15 seconds (0.25 minutes) of the race?

    Test the equation with values from the table.

    b. If the Hare had continued traveling at this rate, how long would it have taken him to complete the 1000 meter race? Would the Hare have won?

    c. How far could the Hare have traveled if he continued at this rate for the entire 50.5 minutes?

The students are all given *The Hopping Hare* handout, and Tara calls on students at random to read the three observations that are known about the Hare's race. After the observations are read, Tara leads the class through a reenactment of the situation. A course is taped on the floor with marks indicating the starting point and the winning post. Since there are three main parts to the Hare's race, the course is split into thirds and the sections marked on the floor. Raphael volunteers to be the Hare. He sprints to the first mark, falls down, and lies there until virtually the whole class starts yelling, "Get up!" "Run!" "Move it!" He jogs the third part of the race. Meanwhile, Tara times Raphael's race using a stopwatch. Kristen records the time and distance on the board as ordered pairs, with the first pair clearly identifying the variables:

Start of race:	(0 seconds, 0 meters) or (0, 0)
Beginning of sleep:	(4, 1.5)
End of sleep:	(27, 1.5)
End of race:	(30, 4)

Tara wants the students to recognize how many meters per second Raphael was traveling during each part of the race. The following dialogue ensues:

Tara: How can we get the Hare's speed during the part of the race before he fell asleep?

Marie: We need to divide distance by time to find the Hare's speed.

Tara: What distance and what time? Come show us.

Marie: We look at (0, 0) to (4, 1.5). To get the distance we do 1.5 meters minus 0, which is 1.5. To get seconds, we do 4 seconds minus 0 and get 4 as the number of seconds to go 1.5 meters. Now, to get speed, we do 1.5 meters divided by 4 seconds to get .375 meters per second.

Tara: What was the Hare's speed for the last part of the race after he woke up? Which ordered pairs do we use?

Tasha: We use (27, 1.5) and (30, 4). Four meters minus 1.5 meters divided by 30 seconds minus 27 seconds. That gives . . . 2.5 meters divided by 3 seconds or .83 meters/sec.

Tara: What about the second part of the race? How fast was Raphael going then?

James: He didn't move because he was sleeping through it, so how could he have had any speed? So his speed was 0.

After finding the speeds for the Hare's race as enacted by Raphael, the students are asked to work together with a neighbor to fill in the first table of *The Hopping Hare* (Figure 10.5) to determine the distances the Hare had traveled by various times. Char and Tara circulate and help students fill in the table. The students find the distances corresponding to the whole minutes fairly easily, but they have difficulty finding the distances associated with the half-minutes.

Tara: Tell me how you filled in your table so far.

Joe: I know 0 minutes is 0 meters. I also know 1 minute is 250 meters because his rate is 250 meters per minute.

Tara: Good. What are you going to put for half a minute?

Joe: Well, half of 250 is 125, right?

Tara: What do you think?

Joe: That's right!

Meanwhile, Char is helping Jessie. Jessie has the first part of the table filled in, but she is struggling with the last part.

Jessie: What do I put for 49.5 minutes?

Char: Think about Raphael's race. Describe the race.

Jessie: He ran fast, slept, then ran faster.

Char: How does Raphael's race relate to the Hare's race?

Jessie: Hare is just waking up at 49.5 minutes because his nap was 47.5 minutes long. He'll be at the same place he was at, 2 minutes, when he went to sleep.

Char then challenges Jessie to think about the last two cells in the table, reminding her that the Hare's rate was 500 meters/second for that part.

Tara and Char constantly refer back to Raphael's acting to get students to remember what had happened in the race. It is evident that when students can refer to Raphael's race, they understand the Hare's race better. Questions like the following are asked of the students to help them understand what the table is asking: "When the Hare woke up, how fast did he travel?" "How far did he go in 0.5 minute?" "How does 0.5 minute compare to a whole minute?"

To help students prepare to graph the data in their table, Tara asks the class, "What do x and y represent in our story?" Justin answers, "The y is the distance, and the x is the time." Tara then asks, "What is the distance measured in, everyone?" The whole class shouts, "Meters!" After completing the Hare's graph, the next step is to discuss the meanings of the change in x and the change in y with respect to the Hare's travel. Tara asks the class questions to summarize the important points from the previous day's activities and to lead into problem 2 of *The Hopping Hare*.

Tara: Can anyone tell me what slope is?

Brandon: Change in x over change in y.

Kristen: No, you mean change in y over change in x.

Tara: How are we going to remember if slope is change in y over change in x or change in x over change in y?

Kelly: Slope is speed like meters/minute.

Marie: And meters is distance—that's our y.

Nick: And minutes is time—that's x.

Tara: So slope is . . .

Brandon: Change in y over change in x.

Tara: And slope and speed are related how?

Kelly: In *The Trodding Tortoise*, every slope we found was the same as the speed.

The students easily determine changes in distance and time, finding corresponding slopes and speeds for the Hare's travels. Questions 3 and 4 in Figure 10.5 are assigned as homework. In question 3, students are to find an equation relating elapsed time and distance for the Hare's first two minutes of travel. In question 4, students are to use the equation to determine the Hare's distance for a few different times and to determine the time it would have taken him to complete the race had he continued to travel at the same speed. For the remaining lessons, students reenact different scenarios to reinforce properties of slope, y-intercept, and their connections to the graph of $y = mx + b$.

ASSESSMENT

As a final assessment, students are asked to write a story interrelating slope, speed and direction of travel, starting position, y-intercept, and the equation of a linear function. Tara uses the cooperative learning technique, Think-Pair-Share, to get students to think and participate in writing original stories about the graphs. She gives them approximately one minute of quiet think time. Next, they are asked to share their story verbally with their partner. This takes about 30 seconds for each story. A lively discussion ensues as students share their stories with their partners.

DISCUSSION AMONG COLLEAGUES

Tara, what is your philosophy of teaching mathematics?

> Students need to be taught using various methods, mainly those that help them investigate how and why things work as they do. They should be encouraged to find answers to questions through opportunities for discovering ideas or rules and testing them out. They need to be asked many questions throughout lessons so that they truly understand the concept behind the material. By asking them thought-provoking questions, we help them to develop self-confidence in their math abilities. Basic skills cannot be forgotten. Tying them into daily lessons is best.

What are the preferred learning styles of your students? How do you accommodate for these styles?

> Most of my students prefer to learn using hands-on activities and visual aids. I use many activities ranging from discovery lessons to cooperative group lessons to get all students involved. Students are taught early how to work in pairs and small groups. I create a comfortable environment, so all students can participate in whole-class discussions and not feel embarrassed or ashamed if they make a mistake. When talking about a given figure or situation, I always have a model or draw a picture. I also allow students to show and explain their work to the entire class on the overhead or white board. This helps them to better understand the material, and it also helps those who are still struggling with the given concept to hear it from a student.

Explain what you do in the lesson in light of the cultural make-up of your students? Are there any teaching practices that you consistently apply based on the culture of your students? Please describe these and give an example of each.

Most students have heard the fable. It seems to be a context that applies universally to all students. To accommodate as many students as possible, we vary activities so that students' various learning styles are utilized: visual, kinesthetic, auditory, and reading/writing. We make certain that students use and translate among various representations: tables, graphs, equations, and stories.

What would you keep and/or change the next time this lesson is taught?

We found students having difficulty completing the tables in Figures 10.3, 10.4, and 10.5. To help the students, we asked questions to help them understand, such as, "When the Hare woke up, how fast did he travel?" "How far did he go in 0.5 minute?" "How does 0.5 minute compare to a whole minute?" In the future, for *The Hopping Hare* we would like to lead the students through graphing and have them fill in the table for the Hare's race simultaneously.

Another change was based on our observations of student behaviors. They were much more reserved the second day and not as focused on the lesson as on day one. We attributed the lack of participation to a schedule change that shortened classes. But we also decided that part of what was missing was physical activity. In seeing how linear functions are created and using the race scenarios of *The Tortoise and the Hare* to do so, students seemed to be better able to sensibly discuss various speeds and directions of travel.

What would you do differently if you taught this lesson to students of a different culture?

Nothing. The activities are culturally unbiased. The mix of the activity, visualization, and oral and written communication gives all students the opportunity to learn.

Tara, what recommendations would you make to a teacher who is about to begin teaching?

Teach students cooperative learning early. Expect them to write often and do homework daily. Encourage and expect students to actively participate in class, and always model the behavior and communication, both written and oral, that is acceptable. Stay organized, be open-minded to new ideas and methods, and keep all students involved. Never allow students to leave your classroom totally frustrated or overwhelmed. Give them something they are confident with to start, and then push further into the concept. Review often, and tie ideas together that have previously been taught.

Char, any other comments?

> *The Tortoise and the Hare* introduces the concepts of slope and inter-
> cept and sets the stage for further development of linear functions,
> which arise throughout school and college mathematics. We recom-
> mend that the activities be followed by a variety of activities that
> apply linear functions in other contexts such as those found in the ref-
> erences (Lappan et al. 1997; Phillips 1991). In addition, we recommend
> that students be encouraged to apply linear functions in contexts
> found in newspapers, almanacs, menus, etc. Linear functions arise in
> a variety of contexts such as grocery ads (buying multiple units), sales
> tax, hourly wages, percentage-off discounts, pizza menus (price com-
> pared with number of toppings), conversions between certain units
> of measure, conversions between monetary units, and calories used
> per minute of activity. Students should be encouraged to complete ex-
> periments such as stacking same-sized items, tying knots in cord,
> hanging same-sized weights from a spring, etc., to experience constant
> rates of change.

COMMENTARY

The three-way collaboration among Char, Tara, and Kara produced an engaging unit that motivated students to solve algebraic problems from an inves-
tigative approach. Through the activities, students discovered the concepts of
slope and y-intercept from experiences with motion by modeling races between
the Tortoise and the Hare. Students discovered that the slope of a line and the
coefficient of the x-term in the equation $y = mx + b$ indicates the rate at which a
character is moving. They also discovered that the starting location of the character, the y-intercept of the graph, and the constant added to the x-term in the
equation of a line all represent the same information. These activities led very
nicely into the formal definitions of slope and y-intercept and their uses in other
situations. The unit is a perfect example of how technology can help make abstract concepts very concrete, dynamic and approachable to students.

The students' attempts to read and create tables, apply and correct their in-
tuitions to interpreting and creating graphs, followed by the development of
equations, is in line with research recommendations for the development of the
function concept. Thornton (2001) notes three approaches to algebra that are
crucial to students' conceptual understanding: developing patterns, using symbols, and applying functions. She writes,

> The power of algebra lies in its capacity to develop and communicate
> insight by representing situations in alternative ways. Whether devel-
> oped through alternative visualizations, symbolic, manipulation, or a

functional approach, each of these alternative representations leads to new insights into mathematical relationships (392).

In this unit, students used multiple approaches for looking at a situation. Throughout they used a functions-and-graph approach for interpreting results and creating their own stories; they used a patterns approach to construct tables and to develop the slope concept; they applied the formal symbolic approach when they determined equations from tables. Most important is the fact that students were able to make connections among these representations as tools for explaining their thinking.

During the learning process, the students made many mistakes. Their misconceptions were addressed through Char's, Tara's, and Kara's skillful questioning and rephrasing, as well as through small group and full class discussion. Students enjoyed and understood the activities that were set in a scenario with which they were familiar. They identified with the context of walking and racing and appreciated the real-life aspect through which they were introduced to linear functions. They learned these powerful mathematical ideas through activities that challenged them to solve problems just as mathematicians do when no ready answer or algorithm is available: They explored and searched for patterns.

Unlike the other profiles in this book, this profile makes no mention of student characteristics. Can readers tell from the unit, or from the students' actions and responses, which dominant culture was represented? Looking to the lesson for clues, one could stretch a guess that the connections to the fables of the Greek philosopher, Aesop, would be of particular interest to Greek or European students. But Aesop's tales are translated into many languages and have become part of many cultures. Yvelyne (first author) grew up thinking that Aesop's tale of *The Ant and the Grasshopper* was a Haitian folk tale because she had heard it many times growing up in a Haitian community. Tara is correct in saying, "Most students have heard the fable. It seems to be a context that applies universally to all students." And for those students who may not have heard it, the lesson begins with the reading of the fable so that all students start with a common understanding.

Assuming that this unit was based on cultural learning styles, do the styles addressed in the unit provide clues to the cultural make-up of Tara's class? In previous chapters we read that kinesthetic or people-oriented activities work well with African Americans and Hispanics. Many Native Americans prefer learning by watching or doing, and many Haitians prefer an oral approach to learning. Cooperative learning is also the strategy most often recommended for diverse cultural groups. However, adhering to the caution not to stereotype groups, the unit incorporates all of these preferences and more. In effect, this unit would very likely motivate students because it begins at a level that students can master. As it proceeds through stages that move from the concrete to the abstract, it does so through a variety of methods. Among the many techniques applied are students' thinking for themselves, getting help from others, using paper and pencil, applying technology, observing a student complete a task, sitting at desks, moving and running across the room to gather data, completing homework, explaining work, listening to the teacher, viewing results on the overhead projector or the board, creating graph stories to share, and working in groups. In short, within the period of this unit, there were aspects to appeal to multiple learning styles.

If we consider the students' work, responses, and involvement in the lesson, then we might guess that the students were at least of average ability for achievement in mathematics. In actuality, the class was a lower-level math class consisting of 26% academic support, 19% special education, and 11% ESL (English as a Second Language) students. The socioeconomic level of students in this class was fairly low with the majority receiving federal assistance for free or reduced-price lunches. Ethnically, the class was primarily Caucasian with two Hispanic students and one Asian student. The students were not among those who enjoyed mathematics. Indeed, as Tara explains,

> The first activity of the school year completed by the class was to write four words relating to mathematics using the initial letters M, A, T, H. The overwhelming majority of students wrote these descriptors: Multiply, Add, Times, and Hate. The last descriptor made it evident that great energy and creativity would be needed to change this attitude. It was a challenging class that needed material presented in ways other than straight from a textbook. Attempts to teach straight from the text resulted in a repeat of teaching the material using hands-on materials the second time through.

The lessons aimed to help students learn the concepts well the *first* time through activities that accommodated their need for intrinsic motivation and a large amount of academic and emotional support. The attention the teachers gave to understanding students' needs helped to make that happen.

The unit is an excellent example of all of the NCTM principles in action because students were taught as college-intending students and were afforded all the tools required to foster higher levels of thinking appropriate to their understanding of important mathematics. For those who believe that calculators are useful only for checking work or are harmful to the development of basic skills, the unit shows a powerful application of technology for providing the foundation for conceptual development of algebraic understanding as well as skills.

Finally, the three-way collaboration between Char, a professor at Grand Valley State University; Kara, who now teaches at Lincoln Christian School in Tulsa, OK; and Tara, a teacher at Creekside Middle School in Zeeland, exemplifies a successful professional relationship built by colleagues to share teaching and assessment strategies for the improvement of students' learning. Such collaboration is at the heart of implementing a culturally responsive pedagogy in the curriculum.

For additional activities with technology coauthored or written by Char and Kara, see Graphs in Real Time, in *Mathematics Teaching in the Middle School 5* (October 1999): 92–99.

CONTACTS

Charlene E. Beckmann
Department of Mathematics
Grand Valley State University
Allendale, MI 49401
Phone: (616) 331-2066
E-mail: beckmannc21@aol.com

Kara D. Rozanski
Lincoln Christian Elementary School
Tulsa, OK 74101-0770
Phone: (918) 664-1820
E-mail: bosalli@aol.com

Tara Maynard
Creekside Middle School
Zeeland, MI 49464
Phone: 616-748-3300
E-mail: tmaymard@zeeland.k12.mi.us

UNIT OVERVIEW:
THE TORTOISE AND THE HARE

Aim: How can we make sense of the meaning of slope and y-intercept for linear functions?

Objectives: Students will accomplish the following:

- Experiment with different walking rates, starting points, and directions of travel to walk various linear and piece-wise linear graphs with the aid of a CBR.

- Complete a table, graph the data, and find a linear equation given a speed and starting point.

- Discover the relationship between slope, speed, and the coefficient of x in a linear equation.

- Discover the relationship between different speeds and directions, and positive, negative, and zero slope.

- Discover the relationship between the starting point, y-intercept, and the value that is added to the x term in the equation of a linear function.

- Translate between representations of table, graph, equation, and scenario.

- Correctly interpret and write stories for graphs that contain both positively and negatively sloped linear segments.

Grade Levels: Sixth to ninth grades

Number of 60-Minute Periods: Five Math periods

Source: Original from Char and Kara with adaptations suggested by Tara and through several pilots with students.

Mathematics Principles and Standards Addressed:

- Principles for equity, curriculum, teaching, learning, technology

- Mathematics as problem solving, communication, connection, representation

- Algebra: Understanding patterns, relations, and functions

- Measurement: Applying appropriate techniques, tools, and formulas to determine measurements

Prerequisites:

- Basic understanding of and ability to work with the Cartesian coordinate plane
- Ability to compile tables or t-charts
- Ability to solve an equation that is in the form of $ax + b = c$
- A limited amount of prior experience graphing motion (especially through the use of motion detectors)

Mathematical Concepts: Students use a CBR to explore and explain the properties for linear and piece-wise linear graphs of distance versus time. They discover properties of slope and y-intercept of a line.

Materials and Tools:

- Per student: handouts, scientific calculators
- Per class: masking tape and meter sticks on floor, stop watch, centimeter measuring tape, CBR (motion detector) and graphing calculator, overhead transparency of coordinate axes or board marked with grid

Management Procedures:

- Preparation of Figures 1–6
- Think-Pair-Share cooperative group work (all students positively interdependent)

Assessment:

- Observation and questioning of students' work (made while circulating the room during class periods)
- Homework
- Final stories using vocabulary learned through the series of activities, which should reflect correct use of vocabulary and deep understanding of the concepts of linear function, constant speed, slope, and y-intercept

11

SUMMARY

I have seen teachers in classrooms across this nation accomplish great things with their students, often in environments that are far from ideal. I have come to believe that the solution to every problem in this world begins with learning and education. It's clear to me that being a teacher is the most important job in the world and that being a mathematics teacher can open doors for students that will change their lives.

Cathy Seely (2004)
2004-2006 NCTM President

CLASSROOM STRATEGIES THAT VALUE MULTICULTURAL STUDENTS

In chapter 3, we (the authors) begin by questioning whether teaching all students in the same way is equitable. The Venn diagram of that chapter serves as a visual for the different methods of teaching as well as a catalyst for some probing questions for which we provide research that shows the merits and pitfalls of both traditional and standards-based teaching methods. The teachers profiled in this book apply reformed-based teaching within a multicultural context and use Gollnick and Chinn's (2002) definition of multicultural education: "Multicultural education is the educational strategy in which students' cultural backgrounds are used to develop effective classroom instruction and school environments." We add that it includes exposing children to other cultures, as well as fostering an understanding and deeper awareness of what is considered fair. The teachers also employ the strategies proposed by Sleeter (1997) for a multicultural classroom. We "see" these strategies as the following:

1. Helping students from historically low-achieving sociocultural groups achieve well in math by using their cultural backgrounds as a resource. (Lynne's students use a Chinese zodiac mat found in the students' neighboring Chinese restaurant; Georgine's students use diabetes, which affects a disproportionate number of Hispanics; Renote's, Diane's, and Samar's students use their heritages; and Char's students use a popular fable.)

2. Opening access to high levels of math for students from historically underrepresented groups. (All the teachers' students, but in particular Tim's students, use trigonometry to calculate the altitude of their rockets; Renote's and Char's students use technology to further higher level processing of ideas.)

3. Teaching mathematics as created in different sociocultural contexts—not just the mathematics of intellectuals of European descent; connecting mathematics to students' lives; and helping students to use math reasoning to think through social or practical issues of concern to them. (All the teachers' methods, but in particular Lynne's use of zodiac signs to develop patterns and concepts of equality and equivalence, Georgine's use of diabetes to study data, and Samar's use of ethnomathematics.)

Such strategies require that the teacher expect, respect, and value the different interpretation that students bring to mathematical problem situations based on the students' cultural interpretation of the problem. Respect for students' ways of thinking or expressions is evident in the teachers' creation of collaborative classroom environments where acceptance of ideas or mistakes is a guide for enhancing learning. The teachers also use different strategies to accommodate different learning styles, and their assessments are authentic and varied.

Most of the math problems posed by the profiled teachers have a cultural connection. Research about Latin American and Korean American children by Hufferd-Ackles, Fuson et al. (2004) shows potential beneficial effects when teachers know about the cultural activities that students bring to the classroom. Their research provides support for "conceptualizing children's activities as contexts that directly influence their arithmetic achievements; ethnicity and other distal variables (e. g., social class and parents' beliefs) influence children's learning by providing access to activities that engage them in particular problems and forms of problem solving" (144). Thus, a primary focus for selecting problems should be on the interests of the multicultural students. This may or may not be the same as problems from multicultural mathematics. Smith and Silver's (1995) work with QUASAR shows that the worthwhile problems that motivate apathetic students to show higher levels of participation need not be of a multicultural nature, but, if they are, that is all the better because students learn about and come to respect people who are different from themselves. From an ethnomathematics perspective, students not only learn about the heritage of other cultures but also, in many cases, come to learn more about their own heritage (e.g., Samar's use of Islamic law as a source of her lesson; Diane's use of heritage quilts; and Renote's uses of the Haitian Revolution).

Indeed, a student can live in a culture and not know a lot about his/her heritage unless encouraged to reflect on it (e.g., Diane's students' interpretation of geometry in the quilt project).

REVISITING QUESTIONS

In chapter 2, preservice teacher Angeline described her daughter Helen and posed an interesting question in her reflection: "Helen's passion lies in social studies and literature. She is not a math-brained child, I guess. Are these children born, not made that way?" Yvelyne's comments to her expressed these thoughts: At the heart of teachers' attempts to reach all students is the belief that all students can be bright in mathematics. The task is to find in what ways our students are smart and how our teaching and assessments can be adjusted to demonstrate and extend their strengths to the area of mathematics. Yvelyne felt this to be true, but on what bases?

IS IT TRUE THAT ALL STUDENTS CAN DO MATHEMATICS?

McGhan (2004) answers a definite "yes" to this question. One reason is his conviction that with effort teachers can make a difference. However, he writes:

> Many will still wonder how this viewpoint squares with reality. They will think something like, "You can't make a cow jump over the Moon just because you want her to." And we can't, because it is certainly true that there are some people who are profoundly mentally handicapped. Estimates usually peg this proportion at about 2%. (This percent can actually increase beyond those with genetic disorders since prenatal conditions [e.g., fetal alcohol syndrome, poor nutrition] and conditions in life [e.g., accidents, abuse] may cause profound mental deficiencies.) At the other end of the human spectrum, there are people like Einstein. . . . So if necessary, we might say there is another 2% or less at the other end of the intellectual spectrum who seem profoundly different from most people. That leaves 96% or more of us who might be just about the same. . . . Whether this model of human capability (it's similar to a model Usiskin [1994] calls the squeezed normal distribution) is accurate is unknown. Here again we can make an existential choice: I choose to believe that there are a few mentally handicapped people in the world, and a few truly gifted people, but that most of us are very much alike in intellectual capacity (3–4).

Colleagues in the Department of Special Education and Habilitative Services at the University of New Orleans would add to McGhan's existential choice. They reason as follows: From a physical perspective, the brains of some students at the bottom portion of the 96% may appear to be severely damaged. However, the extent of cognitive debilitative damage cannot be fully measured by observable behaviors and is therefore difficult to diagnose. There is always the possibility that the assessment tool that was used was inappropriate for that particular individual. They also note that common questions in their field about such students are "When did the student learn that?" and "Did you know that the student could do that?" Because learning occurs over a period of time, the belief that all students can learn is key to the ability to provide all students with the opportunity to reach their potential in any subject. Finally, a flexible curriculum and an assessment process that support all the ways in which people can learn and that allow for individual differences are crucial (Burrell, Miller, and Sharpton 2004). Their recommendations are all represented in the NCTM *Principles and Standards*.

We now come to the first of the eight questions in chapter 3.

DOES ACHIEVING EQUITY IN THE CLASSROOM IMPLY THAT THE TEACHER MUST TAKE INTO ACCOUNT THE CULTURAL PERSPECTIVES OF THE STUDENTS?

From Charlene Beckmann's chapter and the others, we see that lessons engaging students at multiple levels of thinking and interactions rank high in motivating students to learn because of the different learning styles addressed. But does that suffice, or are there students whose culture could cause them to nonetheless be disengaged? From Delpit's (1995a,b) work and others reviewed in chapter 3, we note that home and school expectations may present cultural conflicts for some students in minority cultures. Furthermore, in an article on behavioral patterns and actions typical of diverse groups, McIntyre (1992) lists actions that often result in penalizing or embarrassing students from diverse cultures for what may be mismatches between the students' homes and the school environment. He cites the mismatch as a major cause for the misdiagnoses of behavior disorders among recently arrived immigrants. Teachers who are at risk for reacting in an insensitive manner to students and their cultures often lack appreciation and tolerance for cultural differences. He writes, "These teachers expect their students to adopt majority culture behaviors overnight, denying the validity of centuries of cultural practice" (2). The following are some of the examples of mismatch he lists for different cultures. Based on her experiences growing up in the Haitian culture, Yvelyne adds that group in parentheses where appropriate.

- ◆ Teacher expectation of direct eye contact during disciplinary actions— Eye contact for Asian, African American, and Hispanic children (and Haitians) typically indicates defiance rather than respect.

- ◆ Classroom environments requiring competitive and individualistic goals—They work against the more cooperative learning styles common among Hispanics, African Americans, and Native Americans (and Haitians).

- ◆ Rewarding positive outcomes with checks, gold stars, sweets, and prizes—These are likely to be receptive to the Anglos' more impersonal and materialistic forms of recognition. More personal behaviors such as praise, hugs, pats on the back, or statements like "The family will be proud of your accomplishments" might be more useful for motivating Hispanics, Arabs, and Asians (and Haitians) who wish to bring pride to their families.

♦ Low-income urban youths demonstrate defiant behaviors to a greater extent to avoid being victimized in their tough neighborhoods. Behaviors that include rough language and a greater approval of the use of violence, coupled with learning style differences, are reasons for the high percentages of black youths who get suspended. They receive one-third of the corporeal punishments, are twice as likely as whites to be suspended, and are suspended for longer periods than whites.

♦ Peer pressure often creates high pressure for African Americans, Mexican Americas, Native Hawaiian and Native American youth not to achieve in schools (2–9).

McIntyre addresses two tough questions: How do we teach students school-appropriate behaviors when their actions interfere with educational achievement in the classroom and yet respect their culture? And should we not promote the majority culture so as to prepare students for the expectations of the typical workplace? McIntyre recommends that teacher training institutions assume the role of imparting cultural information. Teachers need to learn about cultural behaviors as well as be aware of their reactions to behaviors of those not like themselves. Given that, he addresses the first question by recommending that schools provide services to culturally diverse students to assist them in becoming "cultural chameleons" capable of displaying "school behavior" when necessary (9). To the second, he admits that it is a difficult decision, but if it is "necessary to teach 'white' behavior, this can be accomplished via specially designed lessons utilizing activities from published social skills curricula. Students should then role-play common situations. Career education lessons that focus on the benefits of being able to display 'office behavior' might also be planned" (9).

Cultural factors also affect assessments. Cultural diversity can be perceived as either a deficit or as a fund of knowledge for building teaching and learning. In her research with other TERC researchers on apparent lack of participation of linguistic-minorities in science classes, Hudicourt-Barnes (2003) shows how these students can be misdiagnosed because of inappropriate assessments. Challenging previous research reporting that Haitian students' interactions in science classes were of poor quality and connected to features of Haitian culture, Hudicourt-Barnes uses the Haitian cultural practice of *bay odyans* (a form of conversational discourse warped with enjoyable argumentation) to engage Haitian students in science discourse. Doing so requires that she facilitate student discourse where they coconstruct and build ideas together. Using this inquiry-based stance, she shows that Haitian students recreating bay odyans in science classrooms actually have a cultural experience that gives them a head start on scientific inquiry. Just as important, given that some tests are put in children's records and later come to reflect their abilities to those viewing the records, her work points to this practice as a risk for continued misdiagnosis of students when cultural factors are not considered.

Thus, to the question of whether it is important to equity for teachers to know of students' cultural backgrounds, the authors say "yes," because, put simply, all students do not need the same thing. Even in a class with apparent homogeneity as in Diane's all-white fourth grade or in Renote's class of all-Haitian literacy students, there is diversity. A second reason for our "yes" answer is that students do not communicate their understanding in the same way. This leads us to questions not posed in chapter 3.

HOW WILL WE KNOW IF ALL STUDENTS ARE LEARNING MATH? WILL NATIONAL TESTS GIVE US THE INFORMATION?

There are always reasons to assess carefully what learning is taking place in mathematics classrooms and to be accountable to stakeholders interested in knowing the results of such assessments. Historically, serious attention to curriculum and assessment in the U.S. education system seems to have been driven by national crises—the Cold War focus on math and science education in the 1950s; the embarrassment of Russia's Sputnik; the report, *A Nation at Risk,* in the early 1980s; and international comparisons like TIMSS in the 1990s. Spasm-like reform movements based on the crisis of the day have too often replaced the necessary, sustained efforts toward steady progress in learning for all students. The claim that the only way we can regain confidence in our schools' effectiveness is to provide evidence that our students surpass those of other countries was articulated by the U.S. governors in their Goals, 2000 proclamation, and their emphasis on rigorous, frequent external tests followed shortly thereafter (U.S. Department of Education, 1994).

Currently, the No Child Left Behind Act (NCLB), signed into law by President Bush in 2002, drives curriculum reform and assessment. The central goal of NCLB is to have all students reach proficient advanced levels of state academic standards in mathematics and reading by 2014. In addition, the act requires states to develop a plan that ensures all teachers are highly qualified by the 2005–06 school year. NCLB requires that each state collect specific data through tests aligned with its standards. New to this law is the requirement that states develop and implement a single statewide accountability system that will ensure all districts and schools make adequate yearly progress (AYP) so that all groups of students reach proficiency or higher in reading and mathematics by 2014 (Gingerich 2003).

From the initiation of the NCLB legislation, proponents and opponents have flooded the news media with their points of view. The arguments are clearly summarized in an article by Mathews (2003) in which he presents differing points of view. From the educators' perspective, he writes,

> The No Child Left Behind law is "out of touch with reality," said Ron Wimmer, school superintendent in Olathe, Kansas, and many of his counterparts across the country agree. Many teachers and principals say they see no way that they can make the required adequate yearly progress toward such daunting goals, given the deadlines. Lawmakers counter that position with "[there is] no other way to make progress, because previous attempts to fix struggling schools with a more modest approach did not work well."

What is NCTM's position on assessments? The NCTM (2000) recommendations for assessment note that

- Assessment should be more than tests.

- Assessments are not merely done *to* students; they are done *for* students, to enhance and guide their learning.

- Assessments should be embedded in instruction, not an interruption in the teaching-learning process.

- Assessment should focus on students' understanding not on just their procedural knowledge.

- Assessment takes many forms.

- Assembling evidence from a variety of sources is more likely to yield an accurate picture.

Mathews (2003) quotes George Miller, who contributed to the writing of the law, as saying, "I look at the angst in the school districts trying to deal with it, the principals trying to deal with it, and I say, 'This is great.' These people are thinking about how to improve the achievement of these children" (2). To this, the authors reply, "LOOK AT THE TEACHERS!" Teachers we see in our work are overburdened, stressed-out, and required to create one paper trail after another (often using their own money to buy these papers) to prove that they are headed toward progress. There is little time built in to facilitate their thinking about their students and to share concerns or ideas. Such conditions are seen as promoting the mathematical abuse of students by NCTM's 2003 President, Johnny Lott (2003), who writes,

> It is legitimate to ask whether students are being abused mathematically, not by the teacher, but by a system that places them in a situation where their cognitive development may be impaired. They may be a

victim of a system that is demanding excellence but providing very few of the resources, both human and physical, that are needed to produce excellence. They may be part of a system that lacks the vision or commitment to pay for what is truly important (3).

CAN HIGH STAKES TESTS PROMOTE EQUITY?

Some educators think not. The increased scores may actually reflect improved scores for students who were close to passing and have been given help to make it through. Thus, weaker students may still be at the bottom. While the test makes it appear as if there is equity in learning, in reality, that may not be the case. It is also very likely that the best teachers are assigned to those students with a chance for passing, again leaving those who need the most help behind. Reys (2004) adds,

> In effect, federal legislation that was intended to improve teacher quality may encourage states to relax standards. Although all teachers will be labeled highly qualified, they may actually be less qualified. But who will know? School superintendents and principals will not be eager to report such information (5).

HOW VALID ARE STANDARDIZED TESTS FOR ENGLISH LANGUAGE LEARNERS?

In her article on high-stakes testing, Valdez Pierce (2003) writes that the public supports such tests for reasons based on the belief that the results indicate how students are doing, that they will make educational systems accountable, and that they will help guide classroom instruction. However, she writes,

> These three assumptions are not necessarily valid for using standardized tests for English Language Learners (ELL) because by their very status, English language learners are in transition to English learning proficiency and are not capable of showing what they know on standardized tests developed for native speakers of English (1).

She sees this as a serious violation of the equity principal because most states are not yet in a financial position for providing ELL with the necessary challenging content or valid assessment. Valid assessments would require 3–5 years to develop and field-test. She stresses that these shortcomings must be conveyed to the general public.

WHAT CAN CLASSROOM TEACHERS DO?

As teachers, we may find our task overwhelming. Not only must we change our thinking about the nature of teaching and learning; we must also be prepared to address the diversity of the students in our classrooms. Many useful strategies are exemplified by the teachers profiled and the issues raised in this book. Other things we can do include becoming members of NCTM and its multicultural affiliates like the North American Study Group on Ethnomathematics, the Benjamin Banneker Association, and *TODOS: Mathematics for All*. We can read reformed-based multicultural articles in journals, participate in conferences and attend other forms of professional development, establish and maintain contacts with other colleagues. We can try, revise, and reflect on lessons; listen to and assess students as a basis for informing instruction; and share views with parents. All of these are key actions that will help to reform teaching and improve student learning. Finally, we must remember that there is no algorithm for a quick and painless change toward reforming our practices. We are not expected to do it alone or to do it all, every day.

WHAT CAN TEACHER EDUCATORS DO?

In addition to the above, assisting preservice and inservice teachers to implement the NCTM reform documents should be a major goal of a teacher preparation program in mathematics education. Leadership classes or workshops to prepare teachers to become the leaders that are envisioned in the reform documents are also necessary. In the past and still today, teachers are handed detailed guidelines adhering closely to a textbook. Shifting from the mind-set of having all the plans "out there" to one where teachers are expected to have input is not automatic or easy. Because they are to facilitate students' learning and engagement in productive planning discussions in their classrooms, teachers need the opportunity to facilitate their own learning as well as the discussions of their peers.

We believe that students have a greater chance of participating in rich mathematical experiences with teachers who understand the content they are teaching; understand the diverse worldviews of mathematics; know the historical sequence of mathematical developments; appreciate how cultures have applied their knowledge of mathematics; and come to know and understand how their students learn. In his review of the research for successfully teaching LEP students, Grant (1992) surmises that it is essential that *all* teachers develop cultural sensitivity and awareness, beginning with their own cultures. This behavior will allow them to work with students from any culture in a manner that shows awareness, acceptance/appreciation, and affirmation of the culture. Teachers must be prepared with the appropriate anthropological and sociological tools so that they can explore and learn about their students' home and community lives in a way that informs without offending their students.

Professional development for both preservice and inservice teachers should thus provide experiences that help teachers develop such skills. Courses that provide time (which may not be available during school hours) for teachers to come together in school teams to vent, discuss, and move toward tackling relevant issues should be offered. Such courses would provide avenues for teachers to construct knowledge that would be based on events from their classroom and related research.

What Can School Administrators Do?

It is important that teachers and administrators work together to devise strategies to move their districts toward implementing culturally sensitive, reform-based changes. To do so, administrators must be aware of reform issues. In addition to the resources cited above, administrators can find supportive services at the national level. For example, school districts that need help to select or implement reformed-based curriculum projects may contact the K–12 Mathematics Curriculum Center. The center offers a variety of products and services to help school districts select and implement curriculum projects funded by the National Science Foundation (NSF) (K–12 Mathematics Curriculum Center, Education Development Center, (800) 332-2429, e-mail: mcc@edc. org).

The history of reform in mathematics education shows that teachers are crucial to reform and that, without their support, educational reform fails—no matter how good the curriculum. Gaining that support requires that teachers be part of the discussion that shapes their professional development programs and that they be given the time to reflect on and to examine their own teaching practice. In addition to specific professional development opportunities, administrators should make it possible for teachers to build time into their schedules to discuss and to reflect on teaching during the school day. Team teaching and collegial coaching should be encouraged to help teachers translate their planning discussions into actual teaching practices. A facilitative leader (teacher or administrator) who can guide discussions toward action focused on curriculum and teaching issues is helpful. Some schools provide such opportunities for teachers by beginning the school day earlier to allow 90 minutes each week for teachers to meet and plan for instruction. Other schools create a schedule in which all teachers at the same grade level have a common planning period. The lesson study process where time during the school day is provided for teachers to collaborate and think deeply about how to help their students gain a conceptual understanding of the content taught could be an ideal situation (Germain-McCarthy, 2001a).

What Can We All Do Together?

Incentives at all levels are necessary to support reform. They can range from a parent who thanks a teacher for taking time to inform the parent of the new curriculum, to a teacher who welcomes a student's insightful comment in the classroom, to an administrator who allows time and compensation for a teacher to move toward a more reflective practice, to the assessment of a policy-maker that a faculty member's work on reform issues is an area that should be included among productivity accomplishments for promotion and tenure decisions. More global incentives, however, require that all of us have a common vision and a coherent plan for implementation that reduces, if not eliminates, conflicting or contradictory messages to members of our professional community. An NSF strategy to promote such coherence is modeled in regions of states that have acquired its systemic initiatives grants. Representatives of stakeholders from all levels of the education community come together to discuss and implement actions conducive to reform. Even without an influx of dollars to spur such a movement, however, local district leaders could start with a smaller piece of the larger puzzle by replicating this process in their own districts.

In addition, Gay (2000) calls for widespread culturally relevant teaching for the following reasons:

> If educators continue to be ignorant of, ignore, impugn, and silence the cultural orientation, values, and performance styles of ethnically different students, they will persist in imposing cultural hegemony, personal denigration, educational inequity, and academic under-achievement upon them. Accepting the validity of these students' cultural socialization and prior experiences will help reverse achievement trends. It is incumbent upon teachers, administrators, and evaluators to deliberately create cultural continuity in educating ethnically diverse students (25).

CONCLUSION

The Venn diagram in chapter 3 helped us to organize and debate ideas on some good questions. Having served that purpose, we review it again, but this time, we redefine Set A to be the set of strategies that teachers use to know their students from different perspectives—strategies derived from conversations with students to learn of culturally relevant material to motivate and enhance their learning. We remind readers that Set B may actually be Set A for those teachers who are mindful of and proficient in implementing *both* methods and who are making choices between the two based on the needs of their students.

The profiles in this book show teachers and students learning new topics through new forms of interaction, evaluating deeper concepts, and addressing more complex problems. As they model how to translate the *Standards* documents into real and workable classroom practices, the teachers also model how to engage students at multiple levels of interaction and understanding. Just as important, the teachers demonstrate a process of teacher-to-student interaction that yields insights into how they might reach multicultural students, and hence, all students.

We wish to remind readers to be mindful that the practices, although based on research, are suggestions that should not be used to limit the learning environments of any group of students or be used to make assumptions about students. We have made no attempt to describe how any particular group behaves because there is too much diversity to do so.

We hope this book helps readers to visualize how the role of a classroom leader can promote an environment that supports all students' creativity. We also hope that while valuing students' diversity, teachers will also share with students the fact that we live in *one* world and that there are numerous commonalities that bind us as *one* people.

APPENDIX A

REFORM-BASED CURRICULUM PROJECTS

Since the publication in 1989 of *The Principles and Standards for School Mathematics* by the National Council of Teachers of Mathematics (NCTM), the thrust of major curriculum development projects has been to develop curriculum consistent with the *Standards*. This Appendix identifies those curriculum projects that have been recognized as models for implementing the standards in mathematics classrooms, sixth through twelfth grades, by the National Science Foundation (NSF).

In 1997, Education Development Center, with funding from NSF, established the K–12 Mathematics Curriculum Center (MCC) to serve school districts in the U.S. interested in mathematics curricula programs consistent with the *Standards*. The Center also provides information and seminars for implementing thirteen comprehensive mathematics programs funded by NSF. For information on the programs listed below, contact MCC at www.edc.org/mcc.

NSF ELEMENTARY PROGRAMS

- ◆ Everyday Mathematics (K–6)
- ◆ Investigations in Number, Data, and Space (K–5)
- ◆ Math Trailblazers (IMS) (K–5)

NSF MIDDLE SCHOOL PROGRAMS

- ◆ Connected Math (6–8)
- ◆ Mathematics in Context (5-8)
- ◆ MathScape: Seeing and Thinking Mathematically (6–8)
- ◆ MATHThematics (STEM) (6–8)
- ◆ Middle School Mathematics Through Applications Project II (6–8)

NSF HIGH SCHOOL PROGRAMS

- Contemporary Mathematics in Context (Core-Plus Mathematics Project) (9–12)

- Interactive Mathematics Project (IMP) (9–12)

- Mathematics: Modeling Our World (ARISE) (9–12)

- MATH Connections: A Secondary Mathematics Core Curriculum (9–12)

- SIMMS Integrated Mathematics: A Modeling Approach Using Technology (9–12)

REFERENCES

Aesop (1954). The Hare and the Tortoise. *Childcraft, Vol. 3, Folk and Fairy Tales*. Chicago, IL: Field Enterprises: 239.

Al-Daffa, A. A. (1977). *The Muslim Contributions to Mathematics*. London: Croom Helm.

American Association for the Advancement of Science: Project 2061. (2003). *Algebra textbook evaluations*. Retrieved October 20, 2003, from, http://www.project2061.org/research/textbook/hsalg/Mathconn/backgrnd.htm.

Ascher, M. (1991). *Ethnomathematics. A Multicultural View of Mathematical Ideas*. Pacific Grove, CA: Brooks/Cole.

Banks, J. A., C. A. Banks, and C. McGee, eds. (1997). *Multicultural Education: Issues and Perspectives*, 3rd ed. Needham Heights, MA: Allyn and Bacon.

Banks, J. (1993). Multicultural education: Development, dimensions, and challenges. *Phi Delta Kappan, 75*(1): 22–28.

Barta, J. (2001). By way of introduction: Mathematics and culture. *Teaching Children Mathematics, 7*(6): 305–311.

Baumgart, K. J. (1989). The History of Algebra. *Historical Topics for the Mathematics Classroom*. Reston, VA: National Council of Teachers of Mathematics: 232–259.

Beckmann, C. (1989). Interpreting graphs. *The Mathematics Teacher, 82*(5): 353–360.

Beckmann, C., and K. Rozanski. (1999, October). Graphs in Real Time. *Mathematics Teaching in the Middle School, 5*(2): 92–99.

Behrend, J. (2001). Are rules interfering with children's mathematical understanding? *Teaching Children Mathematics, 8*(1): 36–42.

Bennett, C. I. (1999). *Comprehensive Multicultural Education: Theory and Practice*, 4th ed. Boston: Allyn & Bacon.

Berggren, J. L. (1986). *Episodes in the Mathematics of Medieval Islam*. New York: Springer-Verlag.

Bishop, A. J. (2001, February). What values do you teach when you teach mathematics? *Teaching Children Mathematics, 7*(6): 346–349.

Boaler, J. (1997). *Experiencing School Mathematics: Teaching Styles, Sex, and Setting*. Buckingham, England: Open Press.

———. (1998). Open and closed mathematics: Students' experiences and understanding. *Journal for Research in Mathematics Education, 29*: 41–62.

———. (2000). Exploring situated insight into research and learning. *Journal for Research in Mathematics Education, 31*(1): 113–119.

———. (2002). Learning from teaching: Exploring the relationship between reform Curriculum and equity. *Journal for Research in Mathematics Education, 33*(4): 239–258.

Boyer, B. C. (1968). The History of Mathematics. John Wiley & Sons.

Bradley, C., and L. Taylor. (2002). Exploring American Indian and Alaskan native cultures and mathematics learning. In *Changing the Faces of Mathematics: Perspectives on Indigenous People of North America*, edited by W. G. Secada. Reston, VA: National Council of Teachers of Mathematics: 49–56.

Bremigan, G. E. (2003). Developing a meaningful understanding of mean. *Teaching Children Mathematics, 9*(1): 22–25.

Bruner, J. (1996). *The Culture of Education.* Cambridge, MA: Harvard University Press.

Burrell, B., J. Miller, T. Pikes, and W. Sharpton. (2004). Conversations with Author. University of New Orleans, LA.

Burrill, G. (1996, July/August). Changing the standards? Oh, no! *National Council of Teachers of Mathematics News Bulletin, 33*(2): 3.

Bustamante, I. M. and B. Travis. (1999). Teachers and students' attitudes towards the use of manipulatives in two predominantly Latino school districts. In *Changing the Faces of Mathematics: Perspectives on Latinos*, edited by L. Ortiz-Franco, N. Hernandes, and Y. De La Cruz. Reston, VA: National Council of Teachers of Mathematics: 81–84.

Carpenter, T., M. Franke, V. Jacob, E. Fennema, and S. Empson. (1998). A longitudinal study of intervention and understanding in children's multi-digit addition and subtraction. *Journal for Research in Mathematics Education, 29*(1): 3–10.

Chapin, S. (1997). The Partners In Change Handbook: A Professional Development Curriculum in Mathematics. Boston: Boston University Press.

Checkley, K., and R. P. Moses. (2001). Algebra and activism: Removing the shackles of low expectations. A conversation with Robert P. Moses. *Educational Leadership, 59*(2): 6–11.

Cobb, P., T. Wood, E. Yackel, et al. (1991). Assessment of a problem-centered second-grade mathematics project. *Journal for Research in Mathematics Education, 22*(1): 3–29.

Cohen, D., and D. L. Ball. (2000, April). Instructional innovation: Reconstructing the story. Paper presented at the annual meeting of the American Educational Research Association, New Orleans, LA.

Damarian, S. K. (2000). Equity, experience, and abstraction: Old issues, new considerations. In *Changing the Faces of Mathematics: Perspectives on Multiculturalism and Gender Equity*, edited by W. G. Secada. Reston, VA: National Council of Teachers of Mathematics: 75–84.

Davidman, L., and P. T. Davidman. (1994). *Teaching with a Multicultural Perspective: A Practical Guide*. New York: Longman.

Davison, D. M. (2002). Teaching mathematics to American Indian students: A cultural approach." In *Changing the Faces of Mathematics: Perspectives on Indigenous People of North America*, edited by W. G. Secada. Reston, VA: National Council of Teachers of Mathematics: 19–24.

Delpit, L. (1995a). Skills and other dilemmas of a progressive Black educator. *Other People's Children: Cultural Conflicts in the Classroom*. New York: The New Press, 11–20.

———. (1995b). The silenced dialogue: Power and pedagogy in educating other people's children. *Other People's Children: Cultural Conflicts in the Classroom*. New York: The New Press, 21–47.

Doherty, R. W., R. S. Hilberg, A. Pinal, and R. G. Tharp. (2002). Five standards and student achievement. *NABE Journal of Research and Practice,* 1(1): 1–24.

Fellows, M., A. Hibner, and N. Koblitz. (1994). Cultural aspects of mathematics education reform. *Notices of the American Mathematics Society,* 41(1): 5–9.

Fensham, P., R. Gunstone, and R. White. (1994). *The Content of Science: A Constructivist Approach to Its Teaching and Learning*. Washington D.C: Falmer Press.

Fuys, D., D. Geddes, and R. Tischler. (1988). The Van Hiele model of thinking in geometry among adolescents. *Journal for Research in Mathematics Education,* Monograph no. 3. Reston, VA: National Council of Teachers of Mathematics.

Fuson, K. C., S. T. Smith, and A. Lo Cicero. (1997). Supporting Latino first graders' ten-structured thinking in urban classrooms. *Journal for Research in Mathematics Education, 28*(6): 738-766.

Fuson, K., W. Carroll, and J. Drueck. (2000). Achievement results for second and third graders using the standards-based curriculum everyday mathematics. *Journal for Research in Mathematics Education, 31*(3): 277–291.

Garcia, M. C. (1993). *Hispanic threads in America*. Retrieved July 26, 2003, from http://www.ma.iup.edu/ Pueblo/latino_cultures/contrib.html.

Garrison, L., and M. J. Kerper. (1999). Adapting mathematics instruction for English-language learners: The language–concept connection. In *Changing the Faces of Mathematics: Perspectives on Latinos*, edited by L. Ortiz-Franco, N. Hernandes, and Y. De La Cruz). Reston, VA: National Council of Teachers of Mathematics: 23–48.

Gay, G. (2000). *Culturally Responsive Teaching: Theory, Research and Practice*. New York: Teachers College Press.

Germain-McCarthy, Y. (1999). *Bringing the NCTM Standards To Life: Best Practices From High Schools*. Princeton, NJ: Eye on Education.

———. (2001a). *Bringing the NCTM Standards To Life: Exemplary Practices From Middle Schools*. Princeton, NJ: Eye on Education.

———. (2001b). The ornamental ironwork of New Orleans: Connection to Haiti and geometry. *Mathematics for the Middle Grades*, 4(7): 430–436.

Goldin, G. A. (1990). Epistemology, constructivism, and discovery learning mathematics. *Journal for Research in Mathematics Education*, Monograph no. 4. Reston, VA: National Council of Teachers of Mathematics: 19–30.

Gingerich, D. (2003, Spring/Summer). No Child Left Behind. *Research for Better Schools Currents*, 6(2): 1.

Gollnick, D. M., and P. C. Chinn. (2002) . *Multicultural Education in a Pluralistic Society*, 6th ed. Upper Saddle River, NJ: Merrill Prentice Hall.

Graham, B. J. (1997). Nature knows its math. In *Marvelous Math: A Book of Poems*, edited by H. B. Lee. New York: Simon & Schuster: 26.

Grant, A. C. (1992). Educational research and teacher training for successfully teaching LEP students. In *Proceedings of the Second International Research Symposium on Limited English Proficient Student Issues: Focus on Evaluation and Measurement, OBEMLA*. National Center for Education Statistics Institute of Education Sciences. Retrieved May 06, 2003, from http://nces.ed.gov/pubs2003/hispanics.

Griggs, S., and R. Dunn. (1996). Hispanic-American students and learning style. In *Eric-EECE Clearinghouse on Elementary and Early Childhood Education*. Retrieved December 16, 2002, from http://ericeece.org/pubs/digest/1996/griggs96.html.

Guberman, S. (2004). A comparative study of children's out-of-school activities and arithmetic achievements. *Journal for Research in Mathematics Education*, 35(2): 117–150.

Gutierrez, R. (1996). Practices, beliefs and cultures of high school mathematics departments: Understanding their influence on student achievement. *Journal of Curriculum Studies*, 28(5): 495–529.

———. (2000). Is the multiculturalization of mathematics doing us more harm than good? *In Multicultural Curriculum: New Directions for Social Theory, Practice, and Policy*, edited by R. Mahalingam and C. McCarthy. London: Routledge.

———. (2002). Enabling the practices of mathematics teachers in context: Towards a new equity research agenda. *Mathematical Thinking and Learning*, 4(2): 145–187.

Haberman, M. (1991). The pedagogy of poverty versus good teaching. *Phi Delta Kappan, 73*(4): 290–294.

Hall, R. (2001, Winter). A Haitian American's view of what teachers and researchers can learn about diverse students' learning. Special joint *Newsletter of National Center for Improving Student Learning and Achievement in Mathematics & Science and Center for Research on Education, Diversity and Excellence, 5*(2): 5–6.

Hankes, J. E., and G. R. Fast. (2002). Investigating the correspondence between Native American pedagogy and constructivist-based instruction. In *Changing the Faces of Mathematics: Perspectives on Indigenous People of North America*, edited by W. G. Secada. Reston, VA: National Council of Teachers of Mathematics: 32–48.

Hastings, E., and D. Yates. (1993). Microcomputer Unit: Graphing Straight Lines. In *Activities for Active Learning and Teaching*, edited by C. Hirsh and R. Laing. Reston, VA: National Council of Teachers of Mathematics: 105–109.

Hernandez, H. (2001). *Multicultural Education: A Teacher's Guide to Linking Context, Process, and Content*, 2nd ed. Upper Saddle River, NJ: Merrill Prentice Hall.

Hess, R., and V. Shipman. (1965). Early experiences and socialization of the cognitive mode in children. *Child Development, 36*(4): 896–886.

Hiebert, J., R. Gallimore, and J. Stigler. (2002). A knowledge base for the teaching profession: What would it look like and how can we get one?" *Educational Researcher, 31*(5): 3–15.

Hiebert, J., R. Gallimore, H. Garnier, et al. (2003). *Teaching Mathematics in Seven Countries: Results from the TIMSS 1999 Video Study*. Washington, DC: U.S. Department of Education, National Center for Education Statistics. Retrieved June 26, 2003, from http://nces.ed.gov/pubs2003/2003013.pdf.

Hollebrands, K. (2004). High school students' intuitive understanding of geometric transformation. *The Mathematics Teacher, 97*(3), 207–214.

Hudicourt-Barnes, J. (2003, Spring). The use of argumentation in Haitian Creole science classes. *Harvard Educational Review 73*(1): 73–93.

Hufferd-Ackles, K., K. Fuson, and G. M. Sherin. (2004). Describing levels of a math-talk community. *Journal for Research in Mathematics Education, 35*(2): 81–116.

Huntley, M., C. Ramaussen, S. J. Villarubi, and J. Fey. (2000). Effects of standards-based mathematics education: A study of the Core-Plus Mathematics Project. *Journal for Research in Mathematics Education, 31*(3): 328–361.

Kafai, Y., and M. Resnick (Eds.). (1996). *Constructionism in Practice: Designing, Thinking, and Learning in a Digital World*. Mahwah, NJ: Lawrence Erlbaum.

Kamii, M. (1990). Opening the algebra gate: Removing obstacles to success in college preparatory mathematics courses. *Journal of Negro Education, 59*(3): 392–406.

Keiser, M., A. Klee, and K. Fitch. (2003). An assessment of students' understanding of angle. *Mathematics Teaching in the Middle School, 9*(2): 116–119.

Khisty, L. (2002). Mathematics learning and the Latino student: Suggestions from research for classroom practice. *Teaching Children Mathematics, 9*(1): 32–35.

Khisty, L., and G. Viergo. (1999). Challenging conventional wisdom: A case study. In *Changing the Faces of Mathematics: Perspectives on Latino and Latinas,* edited by L. Oeriz-Franco, N. Hernandez and Y. De La Cruz, Reston VA: National Council of Teachers of Mathematics: 71–80.

Klein, D. (2001). *Big Business, Race, and Gender in Mathematics Reform.* Retrieved August 1, 2002, from www.mathematicallycorrect.com: 221–232.

Ladson-Billings, G. (1994). *The Dreamkeepers: Successful Teachers of African American Children.* San Francisco: Jossey-Bass.

———. (1995). Making mathematics meaningful in multicultural contexts. In *New Directions for Equity in Mathematics Education,* edited by W. G. Secada, E. Fennema, and L. B. Adajian. New York: Cambridge University Press: 126–145.

———. (1998). It doesn't add up: African American students' mathematics achievement. In Challenges in Mathematics Education of African American Children, edited by C. E. Malloy and L. Brader-Araje. Reston, VA: National Council of Teachers of Mathematics: 7–14.

Lappan, G. (1998, May/June). President's Message Column. *National Council of Teachers of Mathematics News Bulletin, 35*(1): 3.

Lappan, G., W. Fitzgerald, S. Friel, et al. (1997). Variables and patterns. *Connected Mathematics Grade 7.* White Plains, NY: Lawrence Erlbaum Associates.

Lee, H., and W. Jung. (2004). Limited-English-Proficient (LEP) students and mathematical understanding. *Mathematics Teaching in the Middle School, 9*(5), 269–272.

Leonard, J., and S. Guha. (2002). Creating culturally relevance in teaching and learning mathematics. *Teaching Children Mathematics, 9*(2): 114–118.

Lott, J. (2003, April). Students, families, communities, and mathematics teachers. In *National Council of Mathematics Teachers' News Bulletin, 40*(8): 3.

Lubienski, S. (2000). Problem solving as a means for mathematics: An exploratory look through the class lens. *Journal for Research in Mathematics Education, 31*(4): 454–482.

Ma, L. (1999). *Knowing and Teaching Elementary Mathematics*. Mahwah, NJ: Lawrence Erlbaum.

Mack, N. (2001). Building on informal knowledge through instruction in a complex content domain: Partitioning, units, and understanding multiplication of fractions. *Journal for Research in Mathematics Education, 32*(3): 267–295.

Malloy, C. E., and M. G. Jones. (1998). An investigation of African-American students' mathematical problem solving. *Journal for Research in Mathematics Education, 29*(2): 143–163.

Mathews, J. (2003). To educators, "No Child" goals out of reach. *The Washington Post*, Tuesday, September 16. Retrieved September 20, 2003, from http://www.washingtonpost.com/wp-dyn/articles/A15836-2003Sep15.html.

McGhan, B. (2004). *Can it be true that all students can do mathematics?* Retrieved June 15, 2004, from http://comnet.org/cpsr/essays/allearn.htm.

McIntyre, T. (1992). The culturally sensitive disciplinarian. In *Severe Behavior Disorders of Children and Youth Monograph, 15*, 107–115. Retrieved June 22, 2004, from www.maxweber.hunter.cuny.edu/pub/ eres/EDSPC715_MCINTYRE/ C_SenDisp. html 12/23/02.

Means, B. (1997). *Critical Issues: Using Technology to Enhance Engaged Learning for At-Risk Students*. Retrieved June 15, 2004, from http://www.ncrel.org/sdrs/areas/issues/students/atrisk/at400.htm.

Moses, R., M. Kamii, S. McAllister, and J. Howard. (1989). The Algebra Project: Organizing in the spirit of Ella. *Harvard Educational Review, 59*(4): 423–443.

Moskovitch, N. J. (1999). Understanding the needs of Latino students in the reform-oriented mathematics classrooms. In *Changing the Faces of Mathematics: Perspectives on Latinos*, edited by L. Ortiz-Franco, N. Hernandes, and Y. De La Cruz. Reston, VA: National Council of Teachers of Mathematics: 5–12.

National Center for Education Statistics (n.d.). *Trends in International Mathematics and Science Study*. Retrieved August 26, 2003, from http://nces.ed.gov/timss.

National Council of Teachers of Mathematics. (1989). *Curriculum and Evaluation Standards for Learning Mathematics*. Reston, VA: Author.

———. (1991). *Professional Standards for Teaching Mathematics*. Reston, VA: Author.

———. (1995). *Assessment Standard for School Mathematics*. Reston, VA: Author.

———. (2000). *Principles and Standards for School Mathematics*. Reston, VA: Author.

Nieto, S. (1996). *Affirming Diversity*. New York: Longman.

North Central Regional Educational Laboratory. (2004). *21st century skills: Literacy in the digital age*. Retrieved June 21, 2004, from http://www.ncrel.org engauge/skills/skills.htm.

O'Connor, J., and E. Robertson. (2003). *Arabic mathematics: Forgotten brilliance?* Retrieved July 26, 2003, from history.mcs.stand.ac.uk/~history/HistTopics/Arabic_mathematics.html.

Oakes, J. (1985). *Keeping Track: How Schools Structure Inequality.* New Haven, CT: Yale University Press.

Oakes, J. (1990). *Multiplying Inequities: The Effects of Race, Social Class and Tracking on Opportunities to Learn Mathematics and Science.* Santa Monica, CA: Rand Corporation.

Perkins, I., and A. Flor. (2002). Mathematical notations and procedures of recent immigrant students. *Mathematics Teaching in the Middle School, 7*(6): 346–351.

Phillips, E. (1991). *Curriculum and Evaluation Standards for School Mathematics Addenda Series 5–8, Patterns and Functions.* Reston, VA: National Council of Teachers of Mathematics.

Reys, E. R. (2004). A highly qualified mathematics teacher in every classroom by 2005–2006: Blue print or fantasy? *The Mathematics Teacher, 97*(1): 4–5.

Reyes, L. H. (1984). Affective variables and mathematics education. *Elementary School Journal, 84*: 558–581.

Rowser, J. F., T. Y. Koontz. (1995). Inclusion of African American students in mathematics classrooms: Issues of style, curriculum, and expectations. *The Mathematics Teacher, 88*(6): 448–453.

Saul, M. (1997). Common sense: The most important standard. *The Mathematics Teacher, 90*(3): 182–184.

Schmidt, W. H., C. C. McKnight, and S. A. Raizen. (1997). *A Splintered Vision: An investigation of U.S. Science and Mathematics Education.* Boston: Kluwer Academic Publishers.

Schoenfeld, H. A. (2002). Making mathematics work for all children: Issues of standards, testing, and equity. *Educational Researcher, 31*(1): 13–25.

Secada, W. G. (1992). Race, ethnicity, social class, language and achievement in mathematics." In *Handbook of Research in Teaching and Learning,* edited by D. A. Grouws. New York: Macmillan: 623–660.

Seeley, C. (2004, May/June). Coming home. In the *National Council of Teachers of Mathematics News Bulletin, 40*(9):3.

Sharp, J. M. (1999). A teacher-researcher perspective on designing multicultural mathematics experiences for preservice teachers. *Equity and Excellence in Education, 32*(1): 31–42.

Silva, C. M., R. P. Moses, J. Rivers, and P. Johnson. (1990). The Algebra Project: Making middle school mathematics count. *Journal of Negro Education, 59*(3): 375–391.

Silver, E. A., and S. Lane. (1995). Fairness and equity in measuring student learning using a mathematics performance assessment: Results from the QUASAR project. In *Measuring Up: Challenges Minorities Face in Educational Assessment*, edited by A. L. Nettles and M. Nettles. Boston: Kluwer Academic Publishers, 97–120.

Silver, M. S., and E. A. Smith. (1995). Meeting the challenges of diversity and relevance. *Mathematics Teaching in the Middle School, 1*(6): 442–448.

Silver, E. A., M. S. Smith, and B. S. Nelson. (1995). The QUASAR Project: Equity Concerns meet mathematics reform in the middle school. In *New Directions for Equity in Mathematics Education*, edited by W. G. Secada, E. Fennema, and L. B. Adajian. New York: Cambridge University Press: 9–56.

Sleeter, C. E. (1997). Mathematics, multicultural education, and professional development. *Journal of Research in Mathematics Education, 28*(6): 680–696.

Smith, L. B., L. V. Stiff, and M. R. Petree. (2000). Teaching mathematics to the least academically prepared African American students. In *Changing the Faces of Mathematics: Perspectives on African Americans*, edited by W. G. Secada. Reston, VA: National Council of Teachers of Mathematics: 89–96.

Stiff, V. L (2000, November). Learning our lessons. *National Council of Teachers of Mathematics News Bulletin, 37*(4): 3.

———. (2001, December). Status and the status quo—The politics of education. *National Council of Teachers of Mathematics News Bulletin 38*(5): 3.

Struik, D. J. (1967). *A Concise History of Mathematics*, 3rd ed. New York: Dover Publications.

Suzuki, R. H. (1984). Curriculum transformation for multicultural education. *Education and Urban Society, 16*(3): 294–322.

Tate, W. F. (1994, February). Race, retrenchment, and the reform of school mathematics. *Phi Delta Kappan, 75*: 477–485.

———. (1995a). Returning to the root: A culturally relevant approach to mathematics pedagogy. *Theory into Practice, 34*: 166–173.

———. (1995b). Mathematics communication: Creating opportunities to learn. *Teaching Children Mathematics, 1*(6): 344–349, 369.

———. (1997). Race-Ethnicity, SES, gender, and language proficiency trends in mathematics achievement: An update. *Journal for Research in Mathematics Education, 28*(6): 652–679.

Tharp, R. G. (1997). *From At-Risk to Excellence: Research, Theory, and Principles for Practice*. Santa Cruz, CA: Center for Research on Education, Diversity and Excellence, University of California–Santa Cruz.

Torres, A. (2002). Latino identity and politics: Scanning the recent literature. In *Newsletter of the Maurice Gaston Institute for Latino Community Development and Public Policy*. Boston: University of Massachusetts: Winter.

Trafton, P. R., B. J. Reys, and D. G. Wasman. (2001). The math wars—Standards-based mathematics curriculum materials: A phrase in search of a definition. *Phi Delta Kappan, 83*(3): 259–64. Retrieved October 20, 2003. from http://www.pdkintl.org/kappan/k0111tra.htm.

Trumbull, E., S. Nelson-Barber, and J. Mitchell. (2002). Enhancing mathematics instruction for indigenous American students. In *Changing the Faces of Mathematics: Perspectives on Indigenous People of North America*, edited by W. G. Secada. Reston, VA: National Council of Teachers of Mathematics: 1–18.

Usiskin, Z. (1994, Winter). Individual differences in the teaching and learning of mathematics. *University of Chicago School Mathematics Improvement Newsletter, 14*(Winter): 9.

Valdez, P. L. (2003, March/April/May). Accountability and equity: Compatible goals of high-stakes testing? *TESOL Matters Newsletter, 3*(2): 1

Walker, E. N, and L. P. McCoy. (1997). Students' voices: African Americans and mathematics. In *Multicultural and Gender Equity in the Mathematics Classroom: The Gift of Diversity*, edited by J. Trentacosta and M. J. Kenney. Reston, VA: National Council of Teachers of Mathematics: 71–80.

White, D. Y. (2000). Reaching all students mathematically through questioning. In *Changing the Faces of Mathematics: Perspectives on African Americans*, edited by W. G. Secada. Reston, VA: National Council of Teachers of Mathematics: 21-32.

Wiest, L. R. (2001). Teaching mathematics from a multicultural perspective. *Equity and Excellence in Education, 34*(1): 16–25.

Yoshida, M. (1999, April). Lesson study in elementary school mathematics in Japan: A case study. Paper presented at the American Educational Research Association Annual Meeting, Montreal, Canada.

Zaslavsky, C. (1996). *The Multicultural Mathematics Classroom: Bringing in the World*. Portsmouth, NH: Heinemann.

Zaslavsky, C. (1999). *Africa Counts: Numbers and Patterns in African Cultures*. Chicago: Lawrence Hill Books, Review Press.